Manifesting the Promise

"How to Walk in Manifestation"

Tammy Bennett Carter

ROYSTON
Publishing

BK Royston Publishing
P. O. Box 4321
Jeffersonville, IN 47131
502-802-5385
http://www.bkroystonpublishing.com
bkroystonpublishing@gmail.com

© Copyright – 2019

All Rights Reserved. No part of this book may be reproduced, stored in a retrieval system, or transmitted by any means without the written permission of the author.

Cover Layout: Amit Designs and BK Royston Publishing
Cover Image Creation: Dr. Gene Johnson

ISBN-13: 978-1-946111-83-8

Printed in the United States of America

Table of Contents

Introduction — v

Chapter 1: — 1
Our Redemption – "No More Toleration"

Chapter 2: — 27
Sure Promises and "Negotiations"

Chapter 3: — 39
Making Room for the Master – "What are you accommodating?"

Chapter 4: — 47
When God Speaks – "I Need a Revelation"

Chapter 5: — 63
A Quick Work – "Acceleration"

Chapter 6: — 81
God has favored you – "The Visitation"

Chapter 7: — 89
The Fullness of Time – "Manifestation"

Chapter 8: — 103
It's Your Time! – "The Celebration!"

Introduction

Manifesting the Promise (How-to walk-in Manifestation - revised) is a book that will help you to process through areas in your life where strongholds have prevented you from becoming fruitful. These are areas where Satan has gained entrance and ground through various circumstances that have occurred during your lifetime. The Bible speaks about the word of God being a seed sown into different types of grounds; the wayside, stony ground, thorny ground, and good ground. The ground that the Bible is speaking about represents that state of man's heart.

Proverbs 4: 23 – tells us to "guard your heart above all else for it determines the course of your life" (NIV).

It is Satan's desire to use your issues and offences to get you off track, stuck and to take your life down paths that God never intended. Likewise, a healthy heart will establish the right people and the right course, which will bring you into manifestation. Through the help of the Holy Spirit, and the word of God, you must be able to understand what is happening in your life and began to cultivate these areas of your heart so that you can become fruitful. The more you study the word of God the more your ears become attuned to what the Holy Spirit is speaking through God's word. It is my prayer that this book will help you to process from the prophetic utterances that have been spoken over your life into the manifestation of the "promise."

Tammy Carter

Manifesting The Promise

Chapter 1

Our Redemption

"No More Toleration"

"No More Toleration" ... These powerful words came up out of my spirit one day after many months of consecration and bible study. The word toleration comes from the word tolerate which means to allow the existence of, to permit, accept, or condone. God has shown me that one reason we allow the wrong people and things to come into our lives is because we do not know who we really are in Christ. We are the "righteousness of God" in Christ Jesus, we are the head and not the tail, and we are above and not beneath (Deuteronomy 28:13). What are you putting up with, tolerating, enduring, or even allowing that is destroying you and your purpose and causing you to live at a level that is beneath what God has promised?

> *Matthew 16:19 says, "I will give you the keys of the kingdom of heaven, and whatsoever you bind – that is, declare to be improper and unlawful on earth must be already bound in heaven; and whatsoever you loose on earth – declare lawful, must be what is already loosed in heaven. (Amplified)*

Wow! What a word!! God has revealed so many things to me by His Spirit, and this scripture was the basis for that revelation. Many times, we suffer things that we believe are the will of God out of ignorance, thinking that God is getting the glory out of it when He is not. There are many things that we endure, allow, and permit that God never ordained. The point is that we need to pinpoint these areas in our lives and do something about them. Do not expect God to come down and fix things that He has given you the *authority* to fix. The scripture says, "Whatsoever *you* bind shall be bound. God has already done all he is going to do for our situations when He died upon the cross. Now it is our turn to do something, and that something is to use the authority that He has given us. The Word of God lets us know that God has redeemed us from *spiritual death, sickness and poverty (Romans 8:2; Isaiah 53:5; Galatians 3:14)* but how many of us are tolerating these symptoms? Not only do we endure these things, but we also accept those who are being used by the enemy to usher these things into our lives. When we allow the wrong people into our lives, we are robbed of things such as our time, our peace, and a relationship with God which can ultimately affect our spiritual health as well as our natural health. I know I have just said a mouth full but let me give proof to these claims. The scripture I referenced says *"whatsoever you bind,"* that is declared to be improper and unlawful; not your pastor, or your prayer partner, but *you*!

We need to understand that Satan took the authority of this world from Adam through manipulation and deception. Let us take a look at the account of the fall of mankind.

Genesis 3 (NIV) The Fall

1Now the serpent was craftier than any of the wild animals the LORD God had made. He said to the woman, "Did God really say, 'You must not eat from any tree in the garden'?"

2 The woman said to the serpent, "We may eat fruit from the trees in the garden, 3 but God did say, 'You must not eat fruit from the tree that is in the middle of the garden, and you must not touch it, or you will die.'"

4 "You will not certainly die," the serpent said to the woman.

5 "For God knows that when you eat from it your eyes will be opened, and you will be like God, knowing good and evil."

Mankind's desire today is to be like God or be a god and not be accountable to anyone and do as they please. We can clearly see this demonstrated in leadership on every level, in homes, churches, politics, and the world. But God who is a God of order, desires for everyone to be in their rightful places and to be accountable to some authority over them. It is past time for all of mankind to get back in their rightful place starting first in the home. God made man to be the head of the home, but he must first be in subjection to God and his word in order to be effective. Men get back in your rightful places. God created women to be his helper and not a busybody all over the place, but a virtuous woman. Women get back in your places. Children are to be in subjection to their parents and not dictating to their parents or running the home but obedient and respectful. Parents make sure your children are in their rightful places. Without order and accountability there is confusion, chaos and destruction. When mankind went against the order of God through disobedience, a great fall from the place of grace (favor) took place and the earth has not been the same since.

> *6 When the woman saw that the fruit of the tree was good for food and pleasing to the eye, and also desirable for gaining wisdom, she took some and ate it. She also gave some to her husband, who was with her, and he ate it.*

The word of God lets us know that the world is full of the lust of the flesh, the lust of the eyes and the pride of life which does not come from our father God. (*1 John 2:16*). This can be clearly seen in the above scripture as the serpent began to beguile Eve into sinning against God. These are the same strategies the serpent (Satan) is using against us today as he draws those who take his bait further away from God. It is clearly written in the scriptures that God desires that we prosper, but according to His principles as our soul prospers in the knowledge of God (*3 John 2*).

Genesis 3
7 Then the eyes of both of them were opened, and they realized they were naked; so they sewed fig leaves together and made coverings for themselves.

8 Then the man and his wife heard the sound of the LORD God as he was walking in the garden in the cool of the day, and they hid from the LORD God among the trees of the garden.

The shame of their sin and disobedience caused Adam and Eve to hide themselves from God. Guilt and shame alone are not enough to turn us to God but sorrowful repentance for the sins that have separated us from a holy God. When we are caught in our wrongdoing, we are exposed as guilty and then the feelings of shame and humiliation manifest. But there needs to be a godly sorrow as our response to sin. Godly sorrow for our sins requires humility and causes us to not only be sorry, but to change our behavior and posture towards God and man. The word says in *2 Corinthians 7:10 - For godly sorrow worketh repentance to salvation not to be repented of: but the sorrow of the world worketh death.*

The heart of man is in question when there is no sorrow for doing evil. The word of God also lets us know that this would be prevalent in the last days and because of the abundance of iniquity the love of many will become cold (*Matthew 24:12*).

> *9 But the LORD God called to the man, "Where are you?"*

I once did a sermon entitled, "Adam, Where art thou?" (KJV). The whole purpose of asking this question was for the people to self-reflect on where they were in their relationships with God. Where are you today in your relationship with God? "Ye did run well; who did hinder you that you should not obey the truth (Galatians 5:7)?" There are many things that can happen in our lives that will cause us to fall away from following God. We must be honest with ourselves and begin to pinpoint those areas rather than do as Adam and Eve and play the blame game. We must hold ourselves accountable because if we don't God will!

> *10 He answered, "I heard you in the garden, and I was afraid because I was naked; so, I hid."*
> *11 And he said, "Who told you that you were naked? Have you eaten from the tree that I commanded you not to eat from?"*

12 The man said, "The woman you put here with me—she gave me some fruit from the tree, and I ate it."

13 Then the LORD God said to the woman, "What is this you have done?"

The woman said, "The serpent deceived me, and I ate."

14 So the LORD God said to the serpent, "Because you have done this, Cursed are you above all livestock and all wild animals! You will crawl on your belly and you will eat dust all the days of your life.

15 And I will put enmity between you and the woman, and between your offspring and hers; he will crush your head, and you will strike his heel."

16 To the woman he said, "I will make your pains in childbearing very severe; with painful labor you will give birth to children. Your desire will be for your husband, and he will rule over you."

17 To Adam he said, "Because you listened to your wife and ate fruit from the tree about which I commanded you, 'You must not eat from it, "Cursed is the ground because of you; through painful toil you will eat food from it all the days of your life.

18 It will produce thorns and thistles for you, and you will eat the plants of the field.

19 By the sweat of your brow you will eat your food until you return to the ground, since from it you were taken; for dust you are and to dust you will return."

We must realize that there are consequences that come with disobedience. We will always reap what we have sown (Galatians 6:7). Some wisdom that I have learned over the years is that when people get into trouble sometimes, we try to play God by immediately rescuing them without first knowing the back story. Now don't get me wrong, we should always try to help our sisters and brothers but do so using wisdom. Sometimes while trying to pull others out we get pulled into their problems. It is better to be in a position to just give to people without expecting anything in return. Luke 6:35 says, *"But love your enemies, do good to them, and lend to them without expecting to get anything back. Then your reward will be great, and you will be children of the Most High, because he is kind to the ungrateful and wicked."* We should do everything possible to walk in love and keep the peace in relationships, but most of all make sure we are obeying God in the process. The latter part is very important because although Eve felt like she was doing Adam a favor by sharing the fruit, they were both in the process of disobeying God and had to reap severe consequences.

Through means of deceit and because of the disobedience of Adam and Eve, Satan took control of the earth. The authority that was legally given to Adam was lost to Satan. God could not take it right back because it was willfully given over. God is a god of order and his methods are lawful and not lawless. It would have been an illegal act for God to just take back what man handed over to Satan. But God being God, had a plan to redeem mankind through one man, Jesus Christ, God's only son (John 3:16).

> *Romans 5:19-21 (NIV) - 19 For just as through the disobedience of the one man the many were made sinners, so also through the obedience of the one man the many will be made righteous.*

Jesus Christ legally entered the earth through the virgin birth, Mary being his mother. He grew in the wisdom and power of God, became a sacrifice to redeem mankind back to God, arose with all power and gave authority to the church to become the sons of God. Along with that power, we have been also been given the authority of the kingdom to bind and lose. (Matthew 18:18). When did we let the enemy come into our lives to cause us to fall from our place of authority, our place of prayer, reading the word and fasting?

It is time to take inventory of where we are and begin to seek God so that we will know where we are going. The enemy has robbed many of us of time that we should have been spending with God so that we could prepare for our purposes in life. God is asking today, "Where are you in regard to your fellowship with him?" We must be prepared to give God an answer either now or later when we stand before Him.

When we get off track and out of timing, we go down paths that God never intended, meet the wrong people and go through unnecessary suffering. We need to understand that there is a difference between suffering for Christ and suffering ignorantly. The type of suffering that the word of God declared we would have to endure would come through persecution, which means to harass or annoy persistently; to oppress because of one's religion, beliefs, or race (Webster). *II Timothy 3:12 say, "Yea, and all that will live godly in Christ Jesus shall suffer persecution."* There is no scripture that says we are to tolerate sin, sickness, and poverty. Some will say, "Well the Apostle Paul had a thorn in the flesh, and when he asked God to remove it, he would not." Many believe that Paul's thorn in the flesh was a sickness, but the word of God clearly defines Paul's thorn as "the messenger of Satan sent to buffet him."

> *And lest I should be exalted above measure through the abundance of the revelations, there was given to me a thorn in the flesh, the messenger of Satan to buffet me, lest I should be exalted above measure (2 Corinthians 12:7).*

In other words, in order to keep Paul from being prideful because of the abundance of revelations he was receiving, God gave Satan permission to allow Paul to be constantly irritated, frustrated, or harassed (buffeted) in order to keep him humble and relying upon God. So, therefore, God is not going to use sickness to keep us humble because we have been redeemed from the curse of the law, which is spiritual death, sickness, and poverty. Spiritual death came on humanity because of Adam's sin.

> *Romans 5:19-21 says, 19 For as by one man's disobedience many were made sinners, so by the obedience of one shall many be made righteous. 20 Moreover the law entered, that the offence might abound. But where sin abounded, grace did much more abound: 21 That as sin hath reigned unto death, even so might grace reign through righteousness unto eternal life by Jesus Christ our Lord.*

As long as Adam and Eve obediently followed God's laws in the garden, they walked in perfect fellowship with God because there was no sin in their lives. God would meet Adam and Eve in the cool of the day (Genesis 3:8). The 'cool of the day' represented a specific time of the day; speculatively late afternoon or early evening. After they had fallen into sin (disobedience), Adam and Eve were nowhere to be found. Eve allowed Satan to beguile her into eating from the tree of knowledge of good and evil. She also persuaded her husband Adam to do the same. With this sin, came consequences which would cause both to be banished from the garden. Additional consequences would be pain during childbirth for women, and men having to toil to bring forth produce from the ground. The ground would also be cursed and would bring for thorns and thistles (Genesis 3:16-18). Along with the curse, came animosity between Satan and mankind (Genesis 3:15). Although Satan already hated mankind, now, mankind would share that mutual hatred. Ultimately, the seed of the woman would bruise Satan's head and Satan would bruise his (Jesus) heel (Genesis 3:15). This was prophetic of Satan's plot to ultimately kill Jesus but in doing so his kingdom would be destroyed (1 Corinthians 2:7-8). As referenced in the scripture above, 'where sin abounded, grace did much more abound'. Through the death, burial, and resurrection of Jesus Christ, we have been redeemed back to God! But first, we must accept him as our Lord and Savior. Our spiritual birth is predicated upon us confessing with our mouths and believing in our hearts that God has raised Jesus from the dead.

> *Romans 10:9-10 King (KJV) - 9) That if thou shalt confess with thy mouth the Lord Jesus, and shalt believe in thine heart that God hath raised him from the dead, thou shalt be saved.*

10) For with the heart man believeth unto righteousness; and with the mouth confession is made unto salvation.

John 3:3 (KJV) - 3 Jesus answered and said unto him, Verily, verily, I say unto thee, except a man be born again, he cannot see the kingdom of God.

Praise God, we have been redeemed from sin!!! The fall of Adam and Eve also opened the door for sickness and disease, but we were redeemed through Christ sufferings. *Isaiah 53:5 says, "But he was wounded for our transgressions, he was bruised for our iniquities: the chastisement of our peace was upon him; and with his stripes we are healed."* There are those who say that healing is not for us today as it was in the times of the New Testament church. But just as God has not done away with the five-fold ministry gifts, he has not done away with the spiritual gifts. The gift of healing is still in operation in the body of Christ. Healing is not only received through spiritual gifts but through faith in God's word. *Faith comes by hearing and hearing by the word of God* (Romans 10:17). There are many scriptures in the Bible that mention healing. As you begin to meditate on God's word concerning healing your faith is being built up. If the word of God says '*by his stripes you are healed*' (Isaiah 53:5(b)), then if you believe this continually, healing will manifest. The word of God says, *'if we attend unto his word, incline our ear unto his sayings, and keep them amid our hearts, it will be life to those who find them and health to all our flesh'* (Proverbs 4:20-22). God's word is medicine to your flesh! If sickness has not lifted from your body, then increase the dosage of God's word, praise God!

If you believe that God has redeemed you from sickness, do not accept lies from the enemy or anyone who does not believe in divine healing. Satan will try to talk you out of any and every promise that God has given you, including your healing.

We were also redeemed from poverty. Galatians 3:13, 14 say, *"Christ hath redeemed us from the curse of the law, being made a curse for us, for it is written, cursed is everyone that hangeth on a tree, that the blessing of Abraham might come on the Gentiles through Jesus Christ; that we might receive the promise of the Spirit through faith."*

What is the 'blessing of Abraham'? The first promise in Genesis 13: 14 -15, *"The LORD said to Abram after Lot had parted from him, "Look around from where you are, to the north and south, to the east and west. All the land that you see I will give to you and your offspring forever."* The second promise in Genesis 13:16 stated, *"I will make your offspring like the dust of the earth, so that if anyone could count the dust, then your offspring could be counted."* In Genesis 17: 7, a third promise is mentioned where God says to Abraham, *"I will establish my covenant as an everlasting covenant between me and you and your descendants after you for the generations to come, to be your God and the God of your descendants after you."* And lastly, the fourth promise to Abraham in Genesis 22: 18 stated, *"and through your offspring all nations on earth will be blessed, because you have obeyed me."* It is through our obedience to God's word that the blessing of Abraham comes upon us and upon our seed.

If you believe that God has redeemed you from poverty, then there are principles that your life must line up with before you can walk out of poverty into his promise. You must have a heart that is centered on giving with the right spirit, one that is not grudging but liberal. A grudging heart is one that is unwilling to give, grant, or allow; a heart that holds back. Proverbs 15: 25 – *"The liberal soul shall be made fat: and he that watereth shall be watered also himself."* Liberal comes from the word liberate which means to set free, release, let go, let out, or even to come out of slavery or imprisonment. A liberal heart is one that is open, free, with no hang-ups. The word "fat" in this scripture denotes "excess" or "increase." In other words, a person with a liberal heart will come into "excess" or "increase", Glory to God! The remainder of that definition says that "liberal" means to come of out of slavery or imprisonment. Satan can hold you in hostage or imprisonment in your finances because of a lack of giving. Because he knows the principles of God's word, he is able to use your ignorance and disobedience as a strategy. "The thief comes to steal, kill, and destroy", but Christ has come to set you free from the curse. There is only one way out of poverty and that way is through liberal giving and being faithful to the principles of God's word; sowing and reaping. Genesis 8:32 states, *"As long as the earth endures, seedtime and harvest, cold and heat, summer and winter, day and night will never cease." (2 Corinthians 9:6 (KJV) But this I say, He which soweth sparingly shall reap also sparingly; and he which soweth bountifully shall reap also bountifully.* When we began to humble ourselves and do things God's way, then and only then will we see a change in our circumstances, in this case, finances. Either you are obedient or disobedient in regard to God's word; there is no middle ground. God promised to rain on the just as well as the unjust because giving is a principle in God's word. But when He blesses you, your heart will be tested and tried which will reveal whether you are obedient or not.

Relationships: Healthy or Unhealthy

Be careful who you yoke up with once you have come to the light in these areas in your life. Make sure that the people you are around agree with you in these areas of redemption. Wrong relationships can cause these same curses that we have been delivered from, to be ushered right back into our lives. Wrong relationships are unhealthy relationships. To understand what is healthy and what is not, the word of God says that a tree is known by its fruit.

> *Luke 6: 44 - For every tree is known by his own fruit. For of thorns men do not gather figs, nor of a bramble bush gather they grapes.*
>
> *45 A good man out of the good treasure of his heart bringeth forth that which is good; and an evil man out of the evil treasure of his heart bringeth forth that which is evil: for of the abundance of the heart his mouth speaketh.*
>
> *46 And why call ye me, Lord, Lord, and do not the things which I say?*

My understanding of unhealthy relationships came when I recognized patterns in my life. When I was on the path to getting healthy spiritually and emotionally, I would allow people who were "unhealthy" to enter my life. This pattern kept me in a cycle of defeat. I was always in some sort of turmoil, emotionally, spiritually, or financially. The enemy uses these things to steal time, and if he can continue to steal our time, he will ultimately steal our destinies! If you want your life to get on track where the blessings of God are flowing, make sure that you are doing what you need to do to be healthy, your relationships are healthy and that you understand what is going on both in and around you.

People say, "Well you shouldn't judge." Well, not only should you inspect your own fruit from time to time, but the fruit of those who are around you. We are spiritual beings and man is a spirit, he possesses a soul, and lives in a body. (1 Thessalonians 5:23). Paul said that he knows no man after the flesh; *"Wherefore henceforth know we no man after the flesh: yea, though we have known Christ after the flesh, yet now henceforth know we him no more (2 Corinthians 5:17)*. So how are we to know one another? We are to know each other by the spirit. The spirit of a man or woman is the real person. *"The person with the (Holy) Spirit makes judgments about all things, but such a person is not subject to merely human judgments" (1 Corinthians 2:15)*. If people are judging you merely based on your circumstances, and they do not know who you are by the spirit of God, then that is just them being judgmental or critical. If you do not know a person based on who they are in their spirit, then you really do not know them at all.

Stop tolerating what Satan has brought into your life!

> *John 5:1-9 - After this there was a feast of the Jews, and Jesus went up to Jerusalem. Now there is in Jerusalem by the Sheep Gate a pool, which is called in Hebrew, Bethesda, having five porches. In these lay a great multitude of sick people, blind, lame, paralyzed, waiting for the moving of the water. For an angel went down at a certain time into the pool and stirred up the water; then whoever stepped in first, after the stirring of the water, was made well of whatever disease he had. Now a certain man was there who had an infirmity thirty-eight years. When Jesus saw him lying there, and knew that he already had been in that condition a long time, He said to him, "Do you want to be made well? The sick man answered Him, "Sir, I have no man to put me into the pool when the water is stirred up; but while I am coming, another steps down before me. Jesus said to him, "Rise, take up your bed and walk." And immediately the man was made well, took up his bed, and walked.*

This sickness had been governing this man's life for thirty-eight long years! What has been governing your life? For some it may be sin, for some it may be sickness, for some it may be poverty, for some it may be a combination of these things, but we must understand that it was Satan who brought these things about. There is a stirring of the waters taking place; there is a shifting in the spiritual atmosphere.

God is visiting His people in a special way. He has heard the cry of his people and there is a visitation of God on the horizon. God is raising up a people who will help usher in a move of God unlike what has been seen before. His called ones are positioning themselves for a move of God and God will be represented by holiness. Too long has slander, disgrace and compromise been associated with the church. People are going to church praising God and moving through the door into the holy place of the tabernacle but never entering the holy of holies because of contamination. Our churches are filled with emotionalism and religious activity but a lack of the manifested presence of God. Most people have been tolerating these things because they know that they themselves are not right with God. The church must come to a place of repentance because judgement will first begin in the house of God (1 Peter 4:17). The church must no longer conform to the ways of the world but come into agreement with God's word. When we come into agreement with God's word, we can then lay hold on His promises.

God wants to shift you to new levels and dimensions of his glory. If you choose to live on a low level and tolerate whatever Satan brings your way, then do not blame God, it is what you have allowed. The greater the call of God that is on your life, the greater the anointing, the greater the spiritual level, the greater the principality (demon), or the fight that comes against you to stop you from becoming great. You must determine within yourself that "I will not continue to be stopped, stuck, or delayed in my processing on the way to my promise." Begin to declare that "God has a plan laid out in the word of God and if I follow his plan, not mine, I will be fruitful."

> *Psalm 1:3 - And he shall be like a tree planted by the rivers of water, that bringeth forth his fruit in his season; his leaf also shall not wither; and whatsoever he doeth shall prosper.*

Spiritual Maturity

Are you ready to be blessed?

We are living in an age where everything is being shaken and tested, which will prove the value of us all. There is a shifting in relationships. Relationships are being tested!!! As stated earlier, people will either qualify or disqualify themselves when it comes to being part of your life. There is a great need for the church to grow up!!! We need to come out of the works of the flesh that manifests through jealousy, competition, selfishness, usury, backbiting, division, lust, etc.

Galatians 5:19-23 says, "19Now the works of the flesh are manifest, which are these; Adultery, fornication, uncleanness, lasciviousness,

20Idolatry, witchcraft, hatred, variance, emulations, wrath, strife, seditions, heresies,

21Envyings, murders, drunkenness, reveling, and such like: of the which I tell you before, as I have also told you in time past, that they which do such things shall not inherit the kingdom of God.

22But the fruit of the Spirit is love, joy, peace, longsuffering, gentleness, goodness, faith,

23Meekness, temperance: against such there is no law."

God is calling us to spiritual maturity! We must not allow or tolerate the spirit of carnality ruling in our lives. *We must fulfill his joy by being like-minded, having the same love, being of one accord and of one mind. (Philippians 2:2)* The fulfillment of this scripture takes maturity. One way to achieve like-mindedness, the same love, one accord, and being of one mind is to "celebrate" others or put others before ourselves. Our lives should model what we expect of others. If you are in a relationship with a friend or a spouse, you should be willing to give of yourself emotionally, financially, and spiritually as well as receive the same. *Luke 6:38 says, "Give, and it shall be given unto you; good measure, pressed down, and shaken together, and running over, shall men give into your bosom. For with the same measure that ye mete withal it shall be measured to you again."*

We who are leaders in the Body of Christ should be examples of what we expect to see in the body. *1Timothy 4:12 says, "Let no man despise thy youth; but be thou an example of the believers, in word, in conversation, in charity, in spirit, in faith, in purity.* Let us sow the seed that we expect to reap. It takes spiritual maturity to advance you to where you need to be in your walk with God and with others. Sometimes we go through a season of reaping a harvest that should not have been sown but instead of doing the mature thing and repent, we begin to blame others for where we are in life. God is not pleased with our lack of love for each other, or the fact that we tolerate things that he has delivered us from. *"And ye shall know the truth, and the truth shall make you free" John 8:32.* Let us embrace the truth, love the truth, adhere to the truth, celebrate the truth, and not hold the truth as something we dislike. Because, in the truth lies our freedom. If we would truly search our hearts, many of us will find that we are rejecting the truth, hence rejecting Jesus Christ himself!

No More Toleration!! God is calling us into accountability!! Are you tolerating sickness? Have you accepted sickness as your final verdict? You may have become discouraged because you have so long endured your illness. There was a man who had endured an affliction for thirty-eight long years. One day Jesus came and asked him, *"Wilt thou be made whole?" (John 5:6)* In other words, "Do you want to get well?" According to the scripture, Jesus already knew that this man had not only been in this condition for a long time but had been trying to get into the pool for many years to receive his healing. When you have been in a situation, whether sickness or poverty for a long period of time, it can not only affect your thinking, but it can also bring about a sense of despair. Jesus knew that not only did he need to speak to this man's physical condition but to his state of mind.

What words are you speaking?

What words are you speaking? Your words should be faith-filled words, and not words filled with doubt and unbelief. Are you speaking life or are you speaking death over yourself? Your children? Your finances? Your body? Because whatever you are speaking, that is what you will get. *Proverbs 18:21 states, "The tongue has the power of life and death, and those who love it will eat its fruit."* Continue to speak the word over your circumstances and over sickness on a consistent basis. Surround yourself with people who will come into agreement with you and then watch God fulfill His promises to you. Once again, stop tolerating circumstances in your life that are contrary to God's word. You have a choice in the matter, but remember, you decide what you allow, not God. You have the keys to bind and loose. These *keys* are used to move hindrances out of the way so that you will be able to fulfill your God-given purpose.

What are the Keys of the Kingdom?

- A key is a tool that is used to lock or unlock, to allow access or to disallow access. What are your keys?

- Key of Prayer – James 5:16 (b) (Amplified) – *"The heartfelt and persistent prayer of a righteous man (believer) can accomplish much [when put into action and made effective by God—it is dynamic and can have tremendous power]."*

- Key of Praise – 2 Chronicles 20:22 (NIV) *"As they began to sing and praise, the LORD set ambushes against the men of Ammon and Moab and Mount Seir who were invading Judah, and they were defeated."*

- Key of Worship – Acts 16:25-26 (NKJV) *"But at midnight Paul and Silas were praying and singing hymns to God, and the prisoners were listening to them. Suddenly there was a great earthquake, so that the foundations of the prison were shaken; and immediately all the doors were opened, and everyone's chains were loosed."*

- Key of Declarations - Job 22:28 (NKJV) – *"You will also declare a thing, and it will be established for you; So light will shine on your ways."*

Chapter 2

Sure Promises

"Negotiations"

Matthew 5:37: *[37]Simply let your 'Yes' be 'Yes,' and your 'No,' 'No'; anything beyond this comes from the evil one (NIV).* You do not have to *negotiate* with the devil. Webster gives one of the definitions for the word *negotiate* as to get through, around or over successfully. Satan will send people into your life who have the wrong agenda. Some want to have access to your life for all the wrong reasons or talk you out of something that God has told you to do. Let's look at the lives of Jacob and Esau. Esau was a hunter who worked in the fields all day (Genesis 25:27). One day, after working in the fields, Esau found himself so hungry that he felt as though he was at the point of death. Jacob saw this as an opportunity to *negotiate* with Esau. Is it not just like the devil to tempt us when we are at our weakest state? We need to be very careful to whom we reveal our weaknesses. Satan will use people who have wrong motives to take advantage of you. The word of God tells us to beware lest Satan should get an advantage. *2 Corinthians 2:11: [11]Lest Satan should get an advantage of us: for we are not ignorant of his devices.* Just as Jacob saw the opportunity to *negotiate* Esau's desire for food by offering him food (pottage) for his birthright, there are many times Satan will deceive us into accepting less in life or living beneath our privilege because we have negotiated the terms of God's will for our lives. If we will examine our lives and be true to ourselves, we will clearly see where we have compromised. After he was gratified, Esau realized what he had done; he regretted his decision but found no place of repentance.

> *Hebrews 12:16-17:* [16]*Lest there be any fornicator, or profane person, as Esau, who for one morsel of meat sold his birthright.* [17]*For ye know how that afterward, when he would have inherited the blessing, he was rejected: for he found no place of repentance, though he sought it carefully with tears.*

There are some decisions that you make that can cause irreparable damages and Esau's decision was one example. We cannot afford to negotiate the terms of God's will for our lives, no matter who makes the offer. The word says if an angel tried to convince you differently than what God has spoken to you, do not listen, because we know that Satan can transform himself into angel of light *(Ref. 2 Corinthians 11:14-15; Galatians 1:8).*

Although Jacob deceived Esau out of his birthright, his nature was changed from "deceiver" (Jacob means "he grasps the heel" this can also figuratively mean "he deceives") to Israel, which means "one who struggles with God."

From one wrong negotiation, Jacob and Esau's destinies were permanently altered. So, when you are tempted by decisions that will lead to immediate gratifications, know that these decisions come with consequences. You will "reap what you sow."

> *Galatians 6:7-8 says [7]Be not deceived; God is not mocked: for whatsoever a man soweth, that shall he also reap. [8]For he that soweth to his flesh shall of the flesh reap corruption; but he that soweth to the Spirit shall of the Spirit reap life everlasting.*

It is amazing that many people do not believe that this scripture is true until they find themselves in the middle of a situation, and then began to cry out, "why is this happening to me"? As I stated earlier, the word negotiate means to get through, around and over successfully. If you are trying to negotiate by violating God's will for your life, know this, you will not get through, around, or over. The only negotiations that will work are those done legally with the right motives. If you want to get *around* having to spend unnecessary years in the wilderness, you must seek the Lord with your whole heart and be obedient. If you want to get *over* situations that have hindered you and delayed the promises of God, you must fast and pray. There are no shortcuts in God's kingdom and wrongful negotiations will not get you to the blessings of God faster. *Proverbs 10:22 declares, "The blessing of the Lord, it maketh rich, and he addeth no sorrow with it.* Esau got the food he wanted, but it brought great sorrow because it was at the expense of his destiny. Many people have gotten ahead illegally, by negotiating behind closed doors, but what is done in darkness will come to the light.

Another negotiation that went badly was when Judas Iscariot negotiated with the chief priest to betray Jesus. *Matthew 26: [14]Then one of the twelve, called Judas Iscariot, went unto the chief priests, [15]And said unto them, what will ye give me, and I will deliver him unto you? And they covenanted with him for thirty pieces of silver. [16]And from that time he sought opportunity to betray him.* Remember that not all negotiations are born with evil intentions. But the message I am conveying is how we wrongfully negotiate the terms of God's will for our lives, which may ultimately cost us our destinies. In Judas Iscariot's case, his negotiation not only cost him his destiny here on earth, but ultimately his salvation. Negotiations are made in every walk of life; in both business and relationships. I urge you to know the people with whom you are in relationship, whether business or personal. We need to know people by the Spirit of Christ who live in us and the Word of God. *Luke 6:43-45:* *⁴³For a good tree bringeth not forth corrupt fruit; neither doth a corrupt tree brings forth good fruit. ⁴⁴For every tree is known by his own fruit. For of thorns men do not gather figs, nor of a bramble bush gather they grapes. ⁴⁵A good man out of the good treasure of his heart bringeth forth that which is good; and an evil man out of the evil treasure of his heart bringeth forth that which is evil: for of the abundance of the heart his mouth speaketh.* It is during the critical times of negotiation in business and relationships that decisions are made to bring the outcomes of success or failure. Make sure that you are doing business with people who have your best interest at heart. You cannot afford to be in situations that cause you to compromise your integrity, your calling, and put into jeopardy your divine destiny in life. People who have good intentions will keep their word in business or personal dealings. Those who have evil intentions will not hold up their end of the bargain. People with wrong motives will try to negotiate with you in order to remain in your life by making empty promises. Let your no remain no to the devil and let your yes remain yes to God's will. Amos 3:3 says, *"Can two walk together except they be agreed?"* You need to know with whom you are walking. Do not allow people who have wrong motives to enter into any type of allegiance, agreement, or negotiation with you. Stop negotiating with those whose fruit is like their father's, Satan, because his only motive is to steal, kill, and destroy. *John 10:10- "The thief cometh not, but for to steal, and to kill, and to destroy. I am come that they might have life, and that they might have it more abundantly."* What has God called you to do? Coming into agreement with right relationships will allow you to give birth to your purpose. God wants us to be properly positioned so that we produce the right things in the earth. Abraham and Sarah negotiated with Hagar and gave birth to Ishmael and we are still reaping the consequences from this union today in the Middle Eastern wars between the promised son and the bastard son.

> *Genesis 16: 1 – 4 – "Now Sarai Abram's wife bare him no children: and she had a handmaid, an Egyptian, whose name was Hagar.*
>
> *And Sarai said unto Abram, Behold now, the Lord hath restrained me from bearing: I pray thee, go in unto my maid; it may be that I may obtain children by her. And Abram hearkened to the voice of Sarai.*
>
> *And Sarai Abram's wife took Hagar her maid the Egyptian, after Abram had dwelt ten years in the land of Canaan, and gave her to her husband Abram to be his wife.*

And he went in unto Hagar, and she conceived: and when she saw that she had conceived, her mistress was despised in her eyes."

Satan Negotiates with Jesus

Remember that Satan also tried to negotiate with Jesus in the book of *Luke Chapter 4*.

Luke chapter 4. ³"And the devil said unto him, if thou be the Son of God, command this stone that it be made bread. ⁴And Jesus answered him, saying, It is written, That man shall not live by bread alone, but by every word of God. ⁵And the devil, taking him up into a high mountain, showed unto him all the kingdoms of the world in a moment of time. ⁶And the devil said unto him, All this power will I give thee, and the glory of them: for that is delivered unto me; and to whomsoever I will I give it. ⁷If thou therefore wilt worship me, all shall be thine. ⁸And Jesus answered and said unto him, Get thee behind me, Satan: for it is written, Thou shalt worship the Lord thy God, and him only shalt thou serve. ⁹And he brought him to Jerusalem, and set him on a pinnacle of the temple, and said unto him, If thou be the Son of God, cast thyself down from hence: ¹⁰For it is written, He shall give his angels charge over thee, to keep thee: ¹¹And in their hands they shall bear thee up, lest at any time thou dash thy foot against a stone. ¹²And Jesus answering said unto him, It is said, Thou shalt not tempt the Lord thy God. ¹³And when the devil had ended all the temptation, he departed from him for a season."

Jesus was lead into the wilderness by the Holy Spirit to go on a fast for a period of forty days. This was a complete fast, because the scripture mentions that 'in those days he did eat nothing," which also is an indication that he did drink water (Luke 4:2). It is during this time that Jesus goes into intense preparation for the ministry to which he has been called. If Satan could have found a weakness in Jesus he would have stopped him from fulfilling his ministry here on earth. Later, Jesus would declare that the spirit of the Lord was upon him because God has anointed him to preach the gospel, proclaim freedom, recover the sight of the blind, and to set the oppressed free (Luke 4:18). None of this would have been possible if he had failed the test by giving in to temptations and negotiations by Satan in the wilderness. But he was defeated because he could not find any place, cause or occasion within Jesus to tempt or trap him. Here we see three areas of temptation for Jesus which was the same used with Eve in the garden; the lust of the flesh, the lust of the eye and the pride of life (1 John 2:16). The first temptation (the lust of the flesh) was for food; 'command this stone that it be made bread'. Giving in to hunger here would prematurely end the ultimate purpose of the fast which was to push him into his ministry. When God calls us on a fast and gives us instructions, it is not up to us to negotiate the terms but to be fully obedient so that the work God is doing in us can come to completion. Jesus used the word of God to defeat his temptations by saying that man's dependence should not only be for the natural bread, but for God's word. The next temptation was when Satan took Jesus to a high mountain and showed him the kingdoms of the world. In this temptation, he used the lust of eye to tempt Jesus into serving him. Then he promised to give Jesus power in the earth realm (the pride of life) if he would worship him instead of worshipping and serving God. He knew his realm of authority which is why he said in Luke 4:6 (b) "for that is delivered unto me; and to whomsoever I will give it." The reason why Satan could do this is because he had taken the authority that was given to Adam through deceit. After he became the god of this world (2 Corinthians 4:4) he could use the same tactics to beguile and blind the eyes of anyone who will listen to his deceit to keep them from serving God.

> *2 Corinthians 4:4 (KJV) - ⁴ In whom the god of this world hath blinded the minds of them which believe not, lest the light of the glorious gospel of Christ, who is the image of God, should shine unto them.*

Ultimately the negotiations made by Satan were to get Jesus to lose his position by bowing down to him. Here the 'pride of life' can also be seen as an attribute of Satan himself who lost his position in heaven due to pride. But Jesus' stance and position against him can be clearly seen as he resists by telling him that he will only bow down to and worship God. When Satan realized that Jesus was not going to bow down, compromise, negotiate or change his position, he left Jesus for a season. Yes, he leaves us for a season, but then he comes back to test us; and God allows it so that we can be proven and go to our next level. The word of God tells us to 'submit ourselves to God; then resist the devil and he will flee' (James 4:7). When Satan comes to make you compromise through negotiating or altering the terms of what God has spoken to you, make sure your response is no. Let him know that you will not alter or change what God has spoken to you to pacify a temporary issue that can ultimately become a permanent problem through concession. We must stand our ground in faith and not be moved by our current condition. If God says wait on it, fast about it, pray for it, study concerning it, then that alone should be our response and we should not concede until we see the victory. What is Satan using as a bargaining tool in order to gain entrance into your life? Is he using money to gain entrance? Sex? Is he promising you fame? Do not negotiate with him, because you will always lose playing games with the devil. Tell him *"no more negotiations!"*

Right Negotiations

In her deep anguish Hannah prayed to the Lord, weeping bitterly. And she made a vow, saying, "Lord Almighty, if you will only look on your servant's misery and remember me, and not forget your servant but give her a son, then I will give him to the Lord for all the days of his life, and no razor will ever be used on his head." (1 Samuel 1:10-11)

Hannah made a vow or commitment unto the Lord after being barren for many years. The point here is that God allowed Hannah's womb to be closed, because he knew that Hannah, in brokenness of spirit, would humble herself and cry out to him for help. In Hannah's humility, she was positioned to receive what would not only be a blessing to her, but a blessing to the nations, in the child she bore named Samuel. Today, rather than putting our trust in God, we make negotiations with man because we feel that we have no other options. God allows us to be put in situations where we are tested so that ultimately, we will turn to Him. In the bible times, men and women did not have the options we have today, so *by faith*, they had to wait on God. I believe that we are living in a day where circumstances are getting so bad, that *by faith*, we are going to have to trust God to get through perilous times such that have never been seen before. If we keep living, at some point crisis will come to us all. But the question is will you trust God or negotiate with man?

Chapter 3

Making Room for the Master

"What are you accommodating?"

Luke 11:24 say,[24]When the unclean spirit is gone out of a man, he walketh through dry places, seeking rest; and finding none, he saith, I will return unto my house whence I came out. [25]And when he cometh, he finds it swept and garnished. [26]Then goes he, and taketh to him seven other spirits more wicked than himself; and they enter in, and dwell there: and the last state of that man is worse than the first.

When deliverance has taken place in our lives it is God's will that we be filled His Spirit. We cannot choose to take a neutral position in the earth regarding our relationship with God. Either you are going to serve God or you're going to serve Satan. If we do not allow God to fill up voids in our lives, Satan will certainly bring something or someone to fill those places. We need to ask ourselves, who or what is filling up the vacant places in our lives? What are you accommodating? When we give place or make room for Satan, we are accommodating him. The above scripture is referencing a person who has been delivered but remained empty. In other words, this person didn't seek to be filled with the Spirit of God. Have you ever seen people who just went to church to get help but didn't want to commit to God? Maybe this was a person who was tormented by demons and didn't have any peace. Then, after receiving prayer for deliverance, those tormenting spirits went away for a season. But if that same person didn't seek God to remain free by studying God's Word, praying, and listening to praise and worship music, those same spirits, including others with them, came back to reclaim their place in this person's life. The Word of God concludes that the latter state of such a person is worse than their beginning state. This is what happens when you choose to remain neutral after having an encounter with God and the Holy Spirit. We also have to be careful of the kind of environment we are accommodating in our home. In order to do this, we must guard our boundaries by not allowing things such as pornography, violence and strife into our homes. Our minds, eyes, and hearts must be guarded as to what we allow to enter in. These represent portals to which we give access to the things of God or the things of this world.

The presence of God must be ushered back into our homes and in the house of God. Accountability must come first to every leader and believer. Once the presence of God is restored then God's plan for our lives will begin to unfold. We must be guardians over our atmosphere because the word of God tells us that *where envying and strife is, there is confusion and every evil work (James 3:16).* What are you allowing in your home, or for what spirit are you making accommodations? Remember God is not going to come down and set our homes or churches in order, we must do it. Our temples should be charged with the power and presence of God! *Ephesians 5 says, [18]And be not drunk with wine, wherein is excess; but be filled with the Spirit; [19]Speaking to yourselves in psalms and hymns and spiritual songs, singing and making melody in your heart to the Lord; [20]Giving thanks always for all things unto God and the Father in the name of our Lord Jesus Christ [21]Submitting yourselves one to another in the fear of God.* It is time to clean house. The time is now to rid our lives of everything that does not belong in it. The word says the thief comes to steal, kill, and to destroy. We must locate the enemy that is destroying God's presence in our relationships, homes and churches. Locate the enemy that steals valuable time that you should be spending with God. Locate the enemy and rid yourself of these things. Begin to declare, *"No more accommodation"* to Satan, because you are ready to walk in God's favor.

Too Many Distractions

Is it possible that there could be too many distractions in your life? God wants to speak to you but there are too many things going on in and around you. You may need to turn off the television, computer or whatever new technology you have in your home that is causing a distraction. You may just need to meditate on the goodness of God. Begin to fill your time with praise and worship. When is the last time you spent an hour in prayer or yet reading the word of God? Distractions causes delays, interruptions, and come to hinder you from your timing and from birthing out your purpose.

Strength to Give Birth

They told him, "This is what Hezekiah says: This day is a day of distress and rebuke and disgrace, as when children come to the moment of birth and there is no strength to deliver them." (Isaiah 37:3)

The only way that we will be able to give birth in our season is that we learn to create and live in an atmosphere that is always charged with the presence of God. Abortions in our spiritual wombs take place when we allow the wrong things to enter and abide in our presence. The strategy of Satan is to bring stimuli that will ultimately cause miscarriages to our purpose thus hindering us from fulfilling our destinies. The distresses in the above scripture references a time where Hezekiah was so overwhelmed until he was contemplating defeat through giving up. He compared his mental state to that of a woman so exhausted from labor that she does not have the strength to push. But beloved, learn to live in His presence continually, so that when your due season arrives you will have the strength to push forth the vision!

This scripture also references when the Assyrian king, Sennacherib, was threatening to take control of Judah after having already defeated Syria and the northern kingdom of Israel. The field commander also chief cup-bearer referred to as Rab-shakeh came bearing threatening words from Sennacherib, with hopes of intimidating Hezekiah, king of Judah, into giving up. Hezekiah's first response was in the flesh, which was to turn to Egypt for an ally to help fight against this vast army. The prophet Isaiah discouraged this course of action by encouraging Hezekiah and the leaders of Judah to put their trust in the living God! As a result of this encouragement, Hezekiah tore his clothes, put on sackcloth and went into the temple of the Lord *(Isaiah 37:1)*.

David said: Psalms 61:2, "when my heart is overwhelmed, lead me to the rock that is higher than I."

When you are in a situation and you don't know what to do and when the enemy has come against you and there is no one to turn to, talk to God! Let your voice be heard on high! God will hear and He will deliver you!

The next thing that Hezekiah did was to ask the prophet Isaiah to intercede on Judah's behalf. Isaiah's response from God came in *verses 6* and *7*. God let Judah know that the Assyrian king's words were against him, the God of Judah. God also said that He would cause the Assyrian army to return to their own country and there He would cut them down with the sword! The point is, we do not have to accommodate the voice of the enemy in our lives but totally put our trust in God by dwelling in His presence and from this position God will put our enemies to flight!

Compromise

If Satan can cause you to compromise, then accommodations have been made. Compromise is only good when it is based on godly principles. It's dangerous when there is a moral issue at stake. Some have compromised their destinies away by listening to the voice of the enemy. Satan wants to talk you out of becoming who

God created you to be. But you must take your stand against him by abiding in God's presence and listening to His voice.

Chapter 4

When God Speaks

"I Need a Revelation"

Many who are walking in darkness, and do not where they are going, need to hear a word from God. The turning point in your life comes when you get a revelation from Him. The Expanded Vines Expository Dictionary defines the word revelation as: the communication of the knowledge of God to the soul of man; an expression of the mind of God for the instruction of the church.

> *John 12:35-50 - ³⁵Then Jesus said unto them, Yet a little while is the light with you. Walk while ye have the light, lest darkness come upon you: for he that walketh in darkness knows not whither he goes. ³⁶While ye have light, believe in the light, that ye may be the children of light. These things spake Jesus, and departed, and did hide himself from them. ³⁷But though he had done so many miracles before them, yet they believed not on him: ³⁸That the saying of Esaias the prophet might be fulfilled, which he spake, Lord, who hath believed our report? and to whom hath the arm of the Lord been revealed? ³⁹Therefore they could not believe, because that Esaias said again, ⁴⁰He hath blinded their eyes, and hardened their heart; that they should not see with their eyes, nor understand with their heart,*

and be converted, and I should heal them. ⁴¹These things said Esaias, when he saw his glory, and spake of him. ⁴²Nevertheless among the chief rulers also many believed on him; but because of the Pharisees they did not confess him, lest they should be put out of the synagogue: ⁴³For they loved the praise of men more than the praise of God. ⁴⁴Jesus cried and said, He that believeth on me, believeth not on me, but on him that sent me. ⁴⁵And he that sees me sees him that sent me. ⁴⁶I am come a light into the world, that whosoever believeth on me should not abide in darkness. ⁴⁷And if any man hear my words, and believe not, I judge him not: for I came not to judge the world, but to save the world. ⁴⁸He that rejects me, and receives not my words, hath one that judges him: the word that I have spoken, the same shall judge him in the last day. ⁴⁹For I have not spoken of myself; but the Father which sent me, he gave me a commandment, what I should say, and what I should speak. ⁵⁰And I know that his commandment is life everlasting: whatsoever I speak therefore, even as the Father said unto me, so I speak.

We should not be walking in the dark with our spiritual eyes closed, but by the revelation of the spirit of God. It is amazing how many people consistently go to church that not only lack a relationship with God but have no idea how to be led by the spirit of God. They have no direction or instructions from God for their life. These instructions can only be found by dwelling in His presence and by fellowshipping and worshipping God. It is time we walk with our eyes wide open knowing and understanding what the will of God is for our lives. Paul said, that *"the eyes of your understanding may be enlightened that you may know what is the hope of His calling, and what the riches of the glory of his inheritance in the saints, And what is the exceeding greatness of his power to us-ward who believe, according to the working of his mighty power,"* (Ephesians 1:18-19). In verse 37 of John chapter 12, it says that although Jesus performed miracles, they still did not believe in Him. Most people not only fail to recognize a move of God but cannot discern who he is raising up and sending their way for a move of God to take place. That is why the word of God tells us not to know a person by the flesh but to know them by their spirit (2 Corinthians 5:16; Romans 8:16). A lot of religious folk will miss the move of God because they are not willing to sacrifice the things of this world and pay the price to see God's glory. In the Old Testament, every time the man of God (whether prophet, king, or priest) wanted to hear from God an altar was built and a sacrifice was made (Genesis 13:4; Exodus 17:4; 2 Samuel 24:25). How much more must we build an altar and make a sacrifice so that we can hear from God? The purpose of our sacrifices is to bring our flesh under subjection through fasting and prayer. From this position we enter his gates with thanksgiving and into his courts with praise. This leads us to our final posture which is to lay prostrate in the face of a Holy God and wait on him to speak.

> *Romans 12:1-2 (NKJV) - I beseech you therefore, brethren, by the mercies of God, that you present your bodies a living sacrifice, holy, acceptable to God, which is your reasonable service. And do not be conformed to this world, but be transformed by the renewing of your mind, that you may prove what is that good and acceptable and perfect will of God.*

2 Chronicles 7:14 - also gives us the steps of positioning ourselves to hear from God: *"If My people who are called by My name will humble themselves, and pray and seek My face, and turn from their wicked ways, then I will hear from heaven, and will forgive their sin and heal their land."*

> Then Jeremiah 29:13 (NKJV) – says: *"And you will seek Me and find Me, when you search for Me with all your heart."*

So, there is a reason why we are not hearing from God, being led by His Spirit, and receiving revelation from Him. And that reason is that we are not seeking him with our whole heart. We cannot come to God half-hearted and expect him to respond to our prayers. As a result of this approach, our eyes are closed, our minds are darkened and our hearts are not yielded to God. Only the transforming power of His presence can bring about change in our minds and hearts. When we come before him broken in spirit and contrite (repentant) of heart our ears will then open to His voice.

The only way we can remain in the light and knowledge of God's will is that we stay in constant communion with him. How else are we to hear clearly from God unless we remain in his presence? Not only should we stay in fellowship with God, but also it is through our fellowship with Him that we are able to recognize those he has divinely connected to us who will impart into our lives. Jesus walked among those whom he performed great and mighty miracles in the presence of, yet he was rejected by the same. I know that many of us can relate to this fact. Remember when you are being rejected that it's not you that people are rejecting, but Christ. But let's also focus on the positive: those who receive you. I am encouraged by the fact that you don't have to try to make people receive you, but God has a people that will not only receive you, but will also celebrate you. Stop trying to explain yourself to people who will never embrace who God created you to be. Jesus said that many would have ears, but would not be able to hear or understand. He also said that they would have eyes, but would not be able to see or perceive. The reason why many cannot see or hear is because they have not received a revelation from God..."*to whom has the arm of the Lord been revealed?"* (Isaiah 53:1) These are choices that people make inadvertently when they choose to reject you. Stop striving with people trying to get them to receive you by convincing them of who you are in Christ. But rejoice in the fact that God is sending you to a people that will embrace the gift that is inside of you.

Accountability

Before there can be a move of God, there must be a turning back to God through repentance. *Acts 3:19 (NIV) Repent, then, and turn to God, so that your sins may be wiped out, that times of refreshing may come from the Lord.* A lot of what we see today is a display of the flesh and emotions in religious settings. In the news we see leader after leader being exposed for inappropriate behaviors such as infidelity, molestations, and even murder. Another great offense to God is the justification of homosexuality by both church leaders and members. God is holding the church accountable for the sin that is running rampart in His house.

> *1 Peter 4:15 - "For it is time for judgment to begin with God's household; and if it begins with us, what*

will the outcome be for those who do not obey the gospel of God?"

Accountability has come to the body of Christ! Those who are in leadership need to understand first that they are accountable to God. Then there is a need for every leader to have someone that they respect and to whom they can be accountable. No man or ministry should be an island. Not only is this division but this is how cults function. Many have had deplorable acts take place because of a lack of accountability. In the word of God, we see examples of leaders being accountable to one another.

Acts 15 (NIV) The Council at Jerusalem

> *¹ Certain people came down from Judea to Antioch and were teaching the believers: "Unless you are circumcised, according to the custom taught by Moses, you cannot be saved." ² This brought Paul and Barnabas into sharp dispute and debate with them. So, Paul and Barnabas were appointed, along with some other believers, to go up to Jerusalem to see the apostles and elders about this question. ³ The church sent them on their way, and as they traveled through Phoenicia and Samaria, they told how the Gentiles had been converted. This news made all the believers very glad. ⁴ When they came to Jerusalem, they were welcomed by the church and the apostles and elders, to whom they reported everything God had done through them.*
>
> *⁵ Then some of the believers who belonged to the party of the Pharisees stood up and said, "The*

Gentiles must be circumcised and required to keep the Law of Moses." ⁶ The apostles and elders met to consider this question. ⁷ After much discussion, Peter got up and addressed them: "Brothers, you know that some time ago God made a choice among you that the Gentiles might hear from my lips the message of the gospel and believe. ⁸ God, who knows the heart, showed that he accepted them by giving the Holy Spirit to them, just as he did to us. ⁹ He did not discriminate between us and them, for he purified their hearts by faith. ¹⁰ Now then, why do you try to test God by putting on the necks of Gentiles a yoke that neither we nor our ancestors have been able to bear? ¹¹ No! We believe it is through the grace of our Lord Jesus that we are saved, just as they are." ¹² The whole assembly became silent as they listened to Barnabas and Paul telling about the signs and wonders God had done among the Gentiles through them. ¹³ When they finished, James spoke up. "Brothers," he said, "listen to me. ¹⁴ Simon has described to us how God first intervened to choose a people for his name from the Gentiles. ¹⁵ The words of the prophets are in agreement with this, as it is written: ¹⁶ "After this I will return and rebuild David's fallen tent. Its ruins I will rebuild, and I will restore it, ¹⁷ that the rest of mankind may seek the Lord, even all the Gentiles who bear my name, says the Lord, who does these things' ¹⁸ things known from long ago. ¹⁹ "It is my judgment, therefore, that we should not make it difficult for the Gentiles who are turning to God. ²⁰ Instead we should write to them, telling them to abstain from food polluted by idols, from sexual immorality, from the meat of strangled animals and from blood. ²¹ For the Law of Moses has been preached in every city from the earliest times and is read in the synagogues on every Sabbath."

The Council's Letter to Gentile Believers

²² Then the apostles and elders, with the whole church, decided to choose some of their own men and send them to Antioch with Paul and Barnabas. They chose Judas (called Barsabbas) and Silas, men who were leaders among the believers. 23 With them they sent the following letter: The apostles and elders, your brothers, To the Gentile believers in Antioch, Syria and Cilicia:

Greetings.

²⁴ We have heard that some went out from us without our authorization and disturbed you, troubling your minds by what they said. ²⁵ So we all agreed to choose some men and send them to you with our dear friends Barnabas and Paul— ²⁶ men who have risked their lives for the name of our Lord Jesus Christ. ²⁷ Therefore we are sending Judas and Silas to confirm by word of mouth what we are writing. ²⁸ It seemed good to the Holy Spirit and to us not to burden you with anything beyond the following requirements: ²⁹ You are to abstain from food sacrificed to idols, from blood, from the meat of strangled animals and from sexual immorality. You will do well to avoid these things. Farewell.

These "certain people" were Jewish Christians who had come down from Judea to Antioch to teach the Gentile believers about keeping the Law of Moses in order to be saved. They not only did this without authorization by the church but were in error. To make matters worse, they began to argue with two mature leaders, Paul and Barnabas. This is how the church gets out of order. When people who are not mature in their spirits begin to dictate from a place of authority it causes problems. It is up to the mature elders in the church to set things back in order. In this case, Paul and Barnabas were told to get council from the Apostles and elders at the church in Jerusalem. Yet, the question is asked, "Why weren't these issues dealt with sooner rather than later?" The answer is that most of these situations involved leaders who were not accountable to anyone. But what difference does accountability make? Acts Chapter 15 is a demonstration of how problems in the church were resolved by mature leaders who were not only accountable to one another but relied on the Holy Spirit (vs. 28) to direct their counsel concerning difficult decisions.

"The whole assembly became silent as they listened to Barnabas and Paul telling about the signs and wonders God had done among the Gentiles through them" (Acts 15:12). Accountability in the New Testament church came with miracles, signs, and wonders. I believe that it is time for the manifested presence to return back to the house of God in a way that will get the attention of both believers and unbelievers. God used a vision to convince Peter that He was visiting the Gentile nation in a unique way and that

salvation had indeed come to this nation of people. God wants to visit His people more and more in this hour through dreams, visitations and manifestations of His spirit. He also wants His glory restored back into the house of God where we are able, once again to see the miraculous but because of compromise, the glory of God has departed. Churches are filled today with compromise, disunity, competition and entertainment. The Word says it this way, *"having a form of godliness but denying the power thereof: from such turn away"* (2 Timothy 3:5). Now all churches are not this way, but too many are. Part of the great falling away is not that the world is turning away from the church, but the church is turning away from God and have need of repentance and turning back to God for true fellowship and worship.

But God is taking his church back by raising up true worshippers that will lead his people back to the presence of God and into a real relationship. It is not enough to go to church just to say that you went. But it's time for the church to become the true bride of Christ manifested through holiness and without spot or blemish (Hebrews 12:14; Ephesians 5:27). God's promise to His people can be seen in Acts chapter 15 and verses 16 through 17 – *"After this I will return and rebuild David's fallen tent. Its ruins I will rebuild, and I will restore it,* [17] *that the rest of mankind may seek the Lord, even all the Gentiles who bear my name, says the Lord, who does these things."* James was actually quoting prophecy from Amos 9:11-12. These scriptures are prophetic of God visiting His people and not leaving them in ruins: first to the Jew then to the Gentile. This is also a prophetic message to the church, "God will not leave His church in ruins!!" He will visit us yet again, and our latter glory shall be greater than the former (Haggai 2:6-9). The tabernacle of David had in it the Ark of the Covenant which represented the presence and the favor of God for Israel. God is ready to restore His presence and His favor back into His house; but there must be accountability.

Two great instances of accountability as it related to the presence of God were established when God struck Uzzah down for reaching out to stabilize the ark. The ark was about to fall due to the oxen stumbling while being transported but not in compliance with the instructions that had been given by God. David became offended by Uzzah's death, but after seeking God, he was reminded that God had given Moses and Aaron specific instructions on how the ark was to be transported using poles carried by the Levites only and never to be carried upon a cart whether it was old or new (2 Samuel 6:1-7; 1 Chronicles 13:9-12; Exodus 25:12-14; Numbers 7:9). If a move of God is to take place in our churches, leaders must be willing to pay the price by going into the divine presence of God and getting instructions on how to carry out this move. Without God's instructions, the move of God will be aborted in any ministry. The move of God is not about the works of the flesh, because no flesh will glory in His presence.

> *1 Corinthians 1:29-31(NKJV) - that no flesh should glory in His presence. But of Him you are in Christ Jesus, who became for us wisdom from God—and righteousness and sanctification and redemption that, as it is written, "He who glories, let him glory in the LORD.*

Today there are many men and women who are more concerned about statuses and connections than hearing from God. But if you arrive at a high status and position through man and not through God, be careful lest you fall. For the Word says that God gives grace (favor) to the humble, but He resists the proud (James 4:6). If we are to carry a great anointing in the earth, we must be willing to process through the steps that God is giving through constant fellowship in His presence where He speaks to us His instructions and how to carry out His will in the earth.

Another example of accountability that brought immediate judgement is in the New Testament. This account is about Ananias and his wife Sapphira, who experienced immediate judgement because they lied about the price of land that was sold and given to the church. They had made a promise that once their land was sold that they would give all the money to the church. But, instead of giving the entire amount, they held part of it back to keep for themselves (Acts 5:1-9). This was during a time when the church was experiencing a great outpouring of the Spirit of God. Most of the church was unified by one spirit and one heart. Because of this unity, God moved in miraculous ways among the church and every need whether spiritual or material was met. But when Ananias and Sapphira lied and operated in deceitfulness, Peter brought them into accountability, immediately which resulted in their deaths.

With an outpouring of God's spirit upon the church there comes a two-fold manifestation. One sign of a great outpouring is a manifestation of miracle, signs and wonders; and the other is judgement. When we pray and ask God to send revival, we must have a full understanding of exactly what we are asking for. The following should precede a revival:

- Repentance – *Acts 3: 19 – "Repent ye therefore, and be converted, that your sins may be blotted out, when the times of refreshing shall come from the presence of the Lord."*

- Unity – *Acts 2:1-2* – *"And when the day of Pentecost was fully come, they were all with one accord in one place. And suddenly there came a sound from heaven as of a rushing mighty wind, and it filled the entire house where they were sitting."*
- Forgiveness – *Matthew 5:23-24* – *"Therefore, if you are offering your gift at the altar and there remember that your brother or sister has something against you, leave your gift there in front of the altar. First go and be reconciled to them; then come and offer your gift."*

Chapter 5

A Quick Work

"Acceleration"

"For the Lord will execute His word upon the earth, thoroughly and quickly." (NASB - Romans 9:28) "If those days had not been cut short, no one would survive, but for the sake of the elect those days will be shortened." (Matthew 24:22)

Because of the imminence of the coming of the Lord, the days have been shortened and things are accelerating as the time of the gentiles comes to an end *(Luke 21:24)*. The word of God is quickly being fulfilled. Whatever we are going to do for the Lord must be done quickly. When the spirit of the Lord comes upon man, he is able to get things done expeditiously. *I Kings 18:46* (NLT) declares, *"Then the LORD gave special strength to Elijah. He tucked his cloak into his belt and ran ahead of Ahab's chariot all the way to the entrance of Jezreel."* The spirit of the Lord will come upon the church in this last hour to be able to accomplish more than what has been accomplished in the history of the church.

John 14:12 - (KJV) "Verily, verily, I say unto you, He that believeth on me, the works that I do shall he do also; and greater works than these shall he do; because I go unto my Father."

The greater works that Jesus speaks of is that the believer can do greater works as far as 'quantity' and not 'quality.' The reason Jesus referred to the believer being able to do greater works, is because Jesus' ministry was only three years after he went through his preparation in the wilderness. Because we have more time, we should as believers be able to do more works.

> *Joel 2:23 - (KJV) – "Be glad then, ye children of Zion, and rejoice in the Lord your God: for he hath given you the former rain moderately, and he will cause to come down for you the rain, the former rain, and the latter rain in the first month."*

The church can look forward to a great manifestation of God's power in the last days; the former and the latter rain together. This is a double portion of God's power that will come on those who are willing to pay the price. Why so much power? Because we have the knowledge of God from both the Old Testament and the New Testament, we know what it takes to have a move of God because we have understood His word from old! *Habakkuk 2:14* says, *"For the earth will be filled with the knowledge of the glory of the LORD as the waters cover the sea."*

Watch as God begins to accelerate His promises in your life as you position yourself in a place of consecration and obedience. For it is not enough to just fast, pray and read the word, but to move in obedience in the direction that God will take you.

> *Isaiah 1:19-20 - (KJV) "If ye be willing and obedient, ye shall eat the good of the land: But if ye refuse and rebel, ye shall be devoured with the sword: for the mouth of the LORD hath spoken it."*

As you obey God, He has promised to restore all that the enemy has stolen:

> *Joel 2:25-32 - ²⁵ And I will restore to you the years that the locust hath eaten, the cankerworm, and the caterpillar, and the palmerworm, my great army which I sent among you.*
>
> *²⁶ And ye shall eat in plenty, and be satisfied, and praise the name of the LORD your God that hath dealt wondrously with you: and my people shall never be ashamed.*
>
> *²⁷ And ye shall know that I am in the midst of Israel and that I am the LORD your God, and none else: and my people shall never be ashamed.*
>
> *²⁸ And it shall come to pass afterward, that I will pour out my spirit upon all flesh; and your sons and your daughters shall prophesy, your old men shall dream dreams, your young men shall see visions:*
>
> *²⁹ And also upon the servants and upon the handmaids in those days will I pour out my spirit.*
>
> *³⁰ And I will shew wonders in the heavens and in the earth, blood, and fire, and pillars of smoke.*
>
> *³¹ The sun shall be turned into darkness, and the moon into blood, before the great and terrible day of the LORD come.*

³² And it shall come to pass, that whosoever shall call on the name of the LORD shall be delivered: for in mount Zion and in Jerusalem shall be deliverance, as the LORD hath said, and in the remnant whom the LORD shall call.

Even though this scripture is historically speaking about the many battles that Judah went through because of their disobedience, it is also a prophetic work that is parallel to what God will do in the last days. In *verse 26*, God speaks of a time where Judah will experience abundance. In order for God's work to be done "quickly" in the earth, there must be a transfer of wealth to:

1. Visionaries – These leaders are kingdom-minded individuals who have a vision for not only for themselves but for advancing God's people and His kingdom in the earth. *Proverbs 29:18 (AMP) - Where there is no vision [no revelation of God and His word], the people are unrestrained; But happy and blessed is he who keeps the law [of God].*

2. Humanitarians – These are people who have the gift of giving. *Romans 12:6-8 - ⁶ Having then gifts differing according to the grace that is given to us, let us use them: if prophecy, let us prophesy in proportion to our faith; ⁷ or ministry, let us use it in our ministering; he who teaches, in*

teaching; *⁸ he who exhorts, in exhortation;* **he who gives, with liberality**; *he who leads, with diligence; he who shows mercy, with cheerfulness.* An example in the word of God is Cornelius. *Acts 10:1-4 - There was a certain man in Caesarea called Cornelius, a centurion of what was called the Italian Regiment, ² a devout man and one who feared God with all his household,* **who gave alms generously to the people, and prayed to God always.** *³ About the ninth hour of the day he saw clearly in a vision an angel of God coming in and saying to him, "Cornelius!"⁴ And when he observed him, he was afraid, and said, "What is it, lord?" So, he said to him,* **"Your prayers and your alms have come up for a memorial before God.** It wasn't Cornelius's natural status as a centurion that gave him favor with God, but his spiritual status of praying and giving!

3.   Godly Business Men & Women – These are people that God has strategically placed in ministries that will move the vision forward. They will also use their knowledge to help transform the minds of God's people giving them the "power (knowledge) to get wealth!" *Deuteronomy 8:18 - But thou shalt remember the L*ORD *thy God; for it is He that giveth*

thee power to get wealth, that He may establish His covenant which He swore unto thy fathers, as it is this day.

Paradigm Shift

According to the *Merriam-Webster Dictionary*, a *'paradigm shift'* is an important change that happens when the usual way of thinking about or doing something is replaced by a new and different way. This discovery will bring about a *paradigm shift* in our understanding of evolution. The *Cambridge English Dictionary* defines a *paradigm shift* as a time when the usual and accepted way of doing or thinking about something changes completely. These are promises that God has given those who walk with Him: That He will reveal unto us "Secret Things."

1. *Daniel 2:22 (BBE) He is the unveiler of deep and secret things: he has knowledge of what is in the dark, and the light has its living-place with him.*

2. *Luke 8:17 - For nothing is hidden that will not become evident, nor anything secret that will not be known and come to light.*

3.   *Deuteronomy 29:29 - The secret things belong to the LORD our God, but the things revealed belong to us and to our sons forever, that we may observe all the words of this law.*

4.   *Jeremiah 33:3 - Call to Me and I will answer you, and I will tell you great and mighty things, which you do not know.'*

5.   *Luke 12:2-3 - But there is nothing covered up that will not be revealed, and hidden that will not be known.*

6.   *Amos 3:7 - Surely the Lord GOD does nothing Unless He reveals His secret counsel To His servants the prophets.*

7.   *John 15:15 - No longer do I call you slaves, for the slave does not know what his master is doing; but I have called you friends, for all things that I have heard from My Father I have made known to you.*

8.   *1 Corinthians 2:9 - But as it is written: Eye has not seen, nor ear heard, nor have entered into the heart of man the things which God has prepared for those who love Him.*

9. *1 Corinthians 2:10 - For to us God revealed them through the Spirit; for the Spirit searches all things, even the depths of God.*

10. *Ephesians 1:9 - He made known to us the mystery of His will, according to His kind intention which He purposed in Him*

11. *Isaiah 42:16 - And I will bring the blind by a way that they knew not; I will lead them in paths that they have not known: I will make darkness light before them, and crooked things straight. These things will I do unto them, and not forsake them.*

Another part of the acceleration is that God is calling His people out of dead works, which include dead churches and associations. God is positioning His people with divine connections and significant relationships for the purpose of impartation which in turn will accelerate the move of God in the lives of His people. These are relationships that will reciprocate in your life and not just take away from you and drain you of your time. These are God-ordained relationships which will require you to know people by their "spirit" and not by "titles" and "statuses" alone. Many people are not who their "titles" say they are because they have been given these titles and statuses by men and not by God. So, know those who God is connecting you to so that He will be able to redeem the time in your life and accelerate you into the promises that He has given you.

The Lord also let me know that reason for the departure from dead works was because many leaders in local churches have disobeyed God concerning laying foundations and building ministry. When God sent the help that many prayed for these leaders refused to put the sent ones at the foundation. Instead, they proceeded to build the ministry after the flesh based on outward appearance and status. We see this same account happening in the Bible where God told Samuel to go down to the house of Jesse and there, he would anoint the next king to replace Saul.

> *1 Samuel 16:1-13 (NKJV) -- David Anointed King - [1]Now the Lord said to Samuel, "How long will you mourn for Saul, seeing I have rejected him from reigning over Israel? Fill your horn with oil, and go; I am sending you to Jesse the Bethlehemite. For I have provided Myself a king among his sons." [2] And Samuel said, "How can I go? If Saul hears it, he will kill me." But the Lord said, "Take a heifer with you, and say, 'I have come to sacrifice to the Lord.' [3] Then invite Jesse to the sacrifice, and I*

will show you what you shall do; you shall anoint for Me the one I name to you." ⁴ *So Samuel did what the Lord said, and went to Bethlehem. And the elders of the town trembled at his coming, and said, "Do you come peaceably?"* ⁵ *And he said, "Peaceably; I have come to sacrifice to the Lord. Sanctify yourselves, and come with me to the sacrifice." Then he consecrated Jesse and his sons, and invited them to the sacrifice.* ⁶ *So it was, when they came, that he looked at Eliab and said, "Surely the Lord's anointed is before Him!"* ⁷ *But the Lord said to Samuel, "Do not look at his appearance or at his physical stature, because I have refused him. For the Lord does not see as man sees; for man looks at the outward appearance, but the Lord looks at the heart."* ⁸ *So Jesse called Abinadab, and made him pass before Samuel. And he said, "Neither has the Lord chosen this one."* ⁹ *Then Jesse made Shammah pass by. And he said, "Neither has the Lord chosen this one."* ¹⁰ *Thus Jesse made seven of his sons pass before Samuel. And Samuel said to Jesse, "The Lord has not chosen these."* ¹¹ *And Samuel said to Jesse "Are all the young men here?" Then he said, "There remains yet the youngest, and there he is, keeping the sheep." And Samuel said to Jesse, "Send and bring him. For we will not sit down till he comes here."* ¹²*So he sent and brought him in. Now he was ruddy, with bright eyes, and good-looking. And the Lord said, "Arise, anoint him; for this is the one!"* ¹³*Then Samuel took the horn of oil and anointed him in the midst of his brothers; and the Spirit of the Lord came upon David from that day forward.*

Samuel, at first, wanted to anoint Jesse's son Eliab, because of his appearance and stature. Is this not just like leaders today wanting to put people in position because of the way they look and what advantages they appear to have? I have seen this happen in many churches, only for the leader to find out later that the person they put in position had a different (wrong) spirit towards the leader and their ministry and eventually ended up causing strife in the church. But God told Samuel what was most important was 'the heart'. So many times, church leaders overlook those who have the heart of God, a heart for them and the vision, just to put someone in place that they think can move the vision forward.

The latter part of this scripture says, *and the Spirit of the Lord came upon David from that day forward.* From that day forward, the 'move of God' was associated with David. In other words, God would use David to catapult this next 'move of God'. Do we know who God has His hand on in our midst? Many leaders of churches have sensed the move of God upon individuals and have hindered and stopped them because of jealousy. We cannot stop who God chooses to use, but if we try to hinder and stop those who God is raising up, "woe" unto us.

> *Matthew 18:7 (KJV) says, "Woe unto the world because of offences! for it must needs be that offences come; but woe to that man by whom the offence cometh!"*

Man of God, or woman of God operating in the flesh, you cannot stop the move of God and who He chooses to use. Woe unto you if you should try! There is a great online movement in ministry because many have been hindered by leaders in local churches who refuse to get out of God's way. God is a god of divine order and the anointing flows from the head down. It does not flow sideways, it does not flow diagonally, it does not flow from the bottom up, but it flows from the head down. Therefore, God's house needs to be set in order.

> *Psalm 133 - (KJV)* [1] *Behold, how good and how pleasant it is for brethren to dwell together in unity!* [2] *It is like the precious ointment upon the head, that ran down upon the beard even Aaron's beard: that went down to the skirts of his garments;* [3] *As the dew of Hermon, and as the dew that descended upon the mountains of Zion: for there the Lord commanded the blessing, even life for evermore.*
>
> *I Corinthians 12: 28 - And God hath set some in the church, first apostles, secondarily prophets, thirdly teachers, after that miracles, then gifts*

of healings, helps, governments, diversities of tongues.

The scripture says, *and God hath set some in the church*...This is God's doing, and not man. Leaders put God's church in rightful order or release leaders that you cannot come into agreement with. But if you are not going to do things God's way, then close the doors, because if it is not done God's way, there will not be a move of God.

I remember being a Bible teacher at a free-will holiness church at age nineteen. A well-known apostle had been running a revival at our church for a week. During this revival, the apostle began to speak into the life of the pastor and told her to make sure she obeyed God by putting the right people at the foundation of the church. Instead of obeying the word of the Lord, this pastor put who she wanted at the foundation which caused the ministry to shift in the wrong direction. The foundational people that God sent to her, including me, left the ministry. A few years later, this ministry not only became void of the move of God, but the pastor died a premature death.

There are many leaders who are guilty of the same error. Instead of putting the people that God has anointed in position they put whoever they want based on criteria that has nothing to do with what God has said. As a result, these ministries are void of the move of God, out of order and have hindered the ministry of many leaders sent there by God.

The bigger picture is a corporate move of God. A corporate move of God is the effectual working together of all persons in the body of Christ in a spirit of unity and love, in order to accomplish the will of God in the earth. The corporate anointing is activated by the unity of a body of believers, harmoniously functioning together in the realm of the spirit as one. Once God begins to gather together people of a like spirit and mind, it is for the purpose of preparing us for a corporate move. Let us look at the scriptures that either prepares us for a corporate move of God and/or are an example of conditions being right for a corporate move of God to take place.

- *2 Chronicles 5:11-14 – [11]The priests then withdrew from the Holy Place. All the priests who were there had consecrated themselves, regardless of their divisions. [12] All the Levites who were musicians— Asaph, Heman, Jeduthun and their sons and relatives—stood on the east side of the* altar, dressed in fine linen and playing cymbals, harps and lyres. They were accompanied by 120 priests sounding trumpets. [13]The trumpeters and musicians joined in unison to give praise and thanks to the Lord. Accompanied by trumpets, cymbals and other instruments, the singers raised their voices in praise to the Lord and sang: "He is good; his love endures forever. Then the temple of the Lord was filled with the cloud, [14]and the priests could not perform their service because of the cloud, for the glory of the Lord filled the temple of God."

- 2 Chronicles 30:12 - [12]Also in Judah the hand of God was on the people to give them unity of mind to carry out what the king and his officials had ordered, following the word of the LORD.

- Psalms 133:1-3 - Behold, how good and how pleasant it is for brethren to dwell together in unity! [2]It is like the precious ointment upon the head, that ran down upon the beard, even Aaron's beard: that went down to the skirts of his garments; [3]As the dew of Hermon, and as the dew that descended upon the mountains of Zion: for there the LORD commanded the blessing, even life for evermore.

- John 17:23 - I in them and you in me—so that they may be brought to complete unity. Then the world will know that you sent me and have loved them even as you have loved me.

- *Acts 2:1 - And when the day of Pentecost was fully come, they were all with one accord in one place.*

- *Acts 4:31 - And when they had prayed, the place was shaken where they were assembled together; and they were all filled with the Holy Ghost, and they spake the word of God with boldness.*

- *Acts 13:1-3 – [1]Now there were in the church that was at Antioch certain prophets and teachers; as Barnabas, and Simeon that was called Niger, and Lucius of Cyrene, and Manaen, which had been brought up with Herod the tetrarch, and Saul. [2] As they ministered to the Lord, and fasted, the Holy Ghost said, Separate me Barnabas and Saul for the work whereunto I have called them. [3] And when they had fasted and prayed, and laid their hands on them, they sent them away.*

- *Romans 12:4-5 - [4] For as we have many members in one body, and all members have not the same office: [5]So we, being many, are one body in Christ, and everyone members one of another.*

- *Romans 12:16 - Be of the same mind one toward another. Mind not high things, but condescend to men of low estate. Be not wise in your own conceits.*

- *1 Corinthians 1:10 - Now I beseech you, brethren, by the name of our Lord Jesus Christ, that ye all speak the same thing, and that there be no divisions among you; but that ye be perfectly joined together in the same mind and in the same judgment.*

- *1 Corinthians 12:12-13 - ^{12}For as the body is one, and hath many members, and all the members of that one body, being many, are one body: so also, is Christ. ^{13}For by one Spirit are we all baptized into one body, whether we be Jews or Gentiles, whether we be bond or free; and have been all made to drink into one Spirit.*

- *Galatians 3:26-28 - ^{26}For ye are all the children of God by faith in Christ Jesus. ^{27}For as many of you as have been baptized into Christ have put on Christ. ^{28} There is neither Jew nor Greek, there is neither bond nor free, there is neither male nor female: for ye are all one in Christ Jesus.*

- *Ephesians 1:10 - 10 That in the dispensation of the fulness of times he might gather together in one all things in Christ, both which are in heaven, and which are on earth; even in him:*

- *Ephesians 2:14 - For he himself is our peace, who has made the two groups one and has destroyed the barrier, the dividing wall of hostility,*

- *Ephesians 4:3 - Endeavoring to keep the unity of the Spirit in the bond of peace.*

- *Ephesians 4:11-13 - ^{11} And he gave some, apostles; and some, prophets; and some, evangelists; and some, pastors and teachers; ^{12} For the perfecting of the saints, for the work of the ministry, for the edifying* of the body of Christ:*¹³ Till we all come in the unity of the faith, and of the knowledge of the Son of God, unto a perfect man, unto the measure of the stature of the fullness of Christ:*

- *Ephesians 4:16 - From whom the whole body fitly joined together and compacted by that which every joint supplies, according to the effectual working in the measure of every part, makes increase of the body unto the edifying of itself in love.*

- *Philippians 2:1 - If there be therefore any consolation in Christ, if any comfort of love, if any fellowship of the Spirit, if any bowels and mercies,*

- *Colossians 3:13-14 - ¹³ Forbearing one another, and forgiving one another, if any man have a quarrel against any: even as Christ forgave you, so also do ye. ¹⁴ And above all these things put on charity, which is the bond of perfectness.*

- *1 Peter 3:8 - Finally, be ye all of one mind, having compassion one of another, love as brethren, be pitiful, be courteous:*

- *1 John 4:12 - No man hath seen God at any time. If we love one another, God dwelleth in us, and his love is perfected in us.*

Chapter 6

The Visitation

"God Has Favored You"

When God has favored you, He himself will make it known. He will fight your battles; He will go before you; He will anoint you *(You anoint my head with oil, Ps. 23:5)*; and He will visit you. Before there is a manifestation in your life, there must first be a sacrifice, whether it be through fasting and prayer, praise, worship (which speaks of our lifestyle/posture) and/or giving. The word of God calls this sacrifice our reasonable service. The word reasonable denotes that which is fair, equitable or appropriate.

> *Romans 12: 1 – (KJV) I beseech you therefore, brethren, by the mercies of God, that ye present your bodies a living sacrifice, holy, acceptable unto God, which is your reasonable service.*
>
> *Romans 12:1 – (NIV) Therefore, I urge you, brothers and sisters, in view of God's mercy, to offer your bodies as a living sacrifice, holy and pleasing to God--this is your true and proper worship.*

The word of God in the NIV version calls this sacrifice our "proper worship." In other words, sacrificing is a part of worship. It is what's expected from us by God himself. So therefore, in order to get a manifestation from

God, there must first be a sacrifice, but also, even before manifestation, there is yet another event that will take place; visitation. As we search further into the scriptures, we will see that God always visited the promise (manifestation) before manifestation came. By visiting the promise, in other words, God would confirm what He had already promised through some form of visitation. For example, God may have promised you over twenty years ago that he was going to bless you with a home. As time goes by Satan may tell you that God is not going to bless you with a home because it has not manifested as of yet. Nonetheless, God may visit your promise by sending someone to confirm what he said to you years ago through a prophetic utterance to encourage you. In your time of visitation, the word of encouragement may urge you to stay in faith, trust God and continue to sow your seeds because what God has promised will surely come to pass. Understand that God is not locked into to our methodologies. When God first made himself known to me it was through a salvation experience. With Abraham, God made himself known through a promise. Look at some examples in the word of God from both Old and New Testaments. We know that the way mankind approached God was different in the O.T. when compared to the N.T. We can also understand man's approach to God in the O.T.

in the layout of the tabernacle: outer court, inner court, most holy place. Compare this to the three dimensions of man: outer court (body), inner court (soul), most holy place (spirit).

God visits Abraham

As a Bible teacher, when I began to teach on the life of Abraham, I saw a consistent pattern that manifested throughout his life. Whenever Abraham went to a new place, when he wanted to consecrate himself before God and when he wanted to hear from God, he would build an altar.

Genesis 12:8 - [8] and he moved from there to the mountain east of Bethel, and he pitched his tent with Bethel on the west and Ai on the east; there he built an altar to the Lord and called on the name of the Lord.

Genesis 13: 1- 4 – [1] So Abram went up from Egypt to the Negev, with his wife and everything he had, and Lot went with him. [2] Abram had become very wealthy in livestock and in silver and gold. [3] From the Negev he went from place to place until he came to Bethel, to the place between Bethel and Ai where his tent had been earlier [4] and where he had first built an altar. There Abram called on the name of the Lord.

The word "altar" in the Old Testament was a place of "death" and "consecration." This means that Abraham made a sacrifice before calling on the name of the Lord by sacrificing an animal through which he would become consecrated to God.

God visits Jacob

Genesis 32: 24 – 28 - ^{24}And Jacob was left alone; and there wrestled a man with him until the breaking of the day.

^{25}And when he saw that he prevailed not against him, he touched the hollow of his thigh; and the hollow of Jacob's thigh was out of joint, as he wrestled with him.

^{26}And he said, Let me go, for the day breaketh. And he said, I will not let thee go, except thou bless me.

^{27}And he said unto him, What is thy name? And he said, Jacob.

^{28}And he said, Thy name shall be called no more Jacob, but Israel: for as a prince hast thou power with God and with men, and hast prevailed.

Jacob did not just happen to stumble into a blessing, he saw an opportunity to be blessed in the midst of a divine visitation. And even though he didn't know how to go about getting the blessing, by faith, he wrestled with the angel. Because of his persistent faith, he was in position for a breakthrough. It's one thing to prevail with man, but to prevail by faith with God is on a whole different level. When God promotes and blesses you, there's nothing anyone can do about it other than celebrate the blessing and favor upon your life.

God visits Solomon

2 Chronicles 1:6-7 (NKJV) - ⁶And Solomon went up there to the bronze altar before the LORD, which was at the tabernacle of meeting, and offered a thousand burnt offerings on it. ⁷On that night God appeared to Solomon, and said to him, "Ask! What shall I give you?"

We hear a lot about how God asked Solomon what he wanted and how Solomon chose wisdom over riches and after that he became the richest king of all. But what about how he ended up in this place of favor to begin with? According to the word of God, Solomon offered up a thousand burnt offerings; a thousand! That was the most burnt offerings that any king had offered at one time. What a sacrifice! And because of his sacrifice, Solomon received a visitation from God. Yes, God appeared unto Solomon in a vision and asked him, 'what can I give you'? We are constantly asking God for things for one reason or another, and its God's will that we ask. But let me ask you a question, 'what have you done for God lately in your obedience and giving'? Have you made a sacrifice that is pleasing in his sight? We are constantly murmuring and complaining about our lot in life, but by faith we should be praising God for all of His precious promises already given to us by His grace.

Hebrews 13:5 - says, "By him therefore let us offer the sacrifice of praise to God continually, that is, the fruit of our lips giving thanks to his name."

God visits Mary

Luke 1: 26-31 (KJV) - ^{26} *And in the sixth month the angel Gabriel was sent from God unto a city of Galilee, named Nazareth,*

^{27} *To a virgin espoused to a man whose name was Joseph, of the house of David; and the virgin's name was Mary.*

^{28} *And the angel came in unto her, and said, Hail, thou that art highly favored, the Lord is with thee: blessed art thou among women.*

^{29} *And when she saw him, she was troubled at his saying, and cast in her mind what manner of salutation this should be.*

^{30} *And the angel said unto her, Fear not, Mary: for thou hast found favor with God.*

^{31} *And, behold, thou shalt conceive in thy womb, and bring forth a son, and shalt call his name JESUS.*

Mary's visitation from God came in the form of an angel with a message. Mary had found favor with God, but how? It was said that she was 'blessed among all women' to have found this great favor. No doubt, because of her character and lifestyle, she had been closely watched by God. The essence of the purity of her heart came up to God as a sacrifice that was well pleasing. God would never have chosen just any vessel to carry the seed of the son of God.

Once again, our lives should not only be a living sacrifice but a testimony unto God. The word says that *we are epistles written in our hearts read by all men* (2 Cor. 3:2). Mary, like us all, had to receive Jesus as her Lord and savior. The son that she bore would also become her savior who would take away not only her sins but the sins of the world.

God visits Cornelius

Acts 10:1-8 (NKJV) - ¹ There was a certain man in Caesarea called Cornelius, a centurion of what was called the Italian Regiment, ² a devout man and one who feared God with all his household, who gave alms generously to the people, and prayed to God always. ³ About the ninth hour of the day he saw clearly in a vision an angel of God coming in and saying to him, "Cornelius!"

⁴ And when he observed him, he was afraid, and said, "What is it, lord?"

So, he said to him, "Your prayers and your alms have come up for a memorial before God. ⁵ Now send men to Joppa, and send for Simon whose surname is Peter ⁶ He is lodging with Simon, a tanner, whose house is by the sea. He will tell you what you must do." ⁷ And when the angel who spoke to him had departed, Cornelius called two of his household servants and a devout soldier from among those who waited on him continually. ⁸ So when he had explained all these things to them, he sent them to Joppa.

Cornelius's liberal giving, consistent prayers and fasting were a sacrifice that was well pleasing to God and because of this he received a special visitation. This is one of the most phenomenal accounts in the word of God. Here is a gentile who worshipped God in a time where the apostles were primarily preaching the gospel to the Jews. God had to prepare the heart of Simon Peter to take this gospel message to Cornelius's house. When Simon Peter stood up to preach this gospel message, the Holy Ghost fell amongst them all confirming that God was well pleased.

I encourage you to be faithful to God. He is aligning you with the right set of circumstances and relationships so that He can bring you into the promise (manifestation). There are relationships that must go and there are relationships that must come. We are commanded to know people by the spirit and not by the flesh so that we don't miss the visitation right before manifestation.

Chapter 7

The Fullness of Time

"Manifestation"

Romans 8:19, 22 - For the earnest expectation of the creature waits for the manifestation of the sons of God. ^{22}For we know that the whole creation groans and travails in pain together until now.

The word "manifest" means to make evident or certain by showing or displaying. Another definition of the word "manifest" or "manifestation" is *a public demonstration of power and purpose.* WOW! God is positioning you to bring you into all that he has promised you in order to give you a public demonstration of his power and purpose in your life. The purpose of the moaning, groaning, travailing, frustrations, failures, highs and lows is to properly position us into a place where we can hear his voice and understand His will concerning us. God wants to position you, so that when he pours out of his spirit both spiritual blessings and natural blessings, you will be in a place that He called you to be in, in order to receive. It is God's desire to bring us into the fulfillment of His will for our lives. But we must "know Him" as the Apostle Paul said in the word of God, not only in the power of his resurrection but also in the fellowship of his sufferings.

Philippians 3: 10, 12 - That I may know him, and the power of his resurrection, and the fellowship of his sufferings, being made conformable unto his death; Not as though I had already attained, either were already perfect: but I follow after, if that I may apprehend that for which also I am apprehended of Christ Jesus.

To 'know Christ' is to understand how he moves and when he moves; also, to understand and know when he is speaking. To 'know Him' also means to become intimately acquainted with him. We understand this concept as it relates to a husband and wife. You know that in order to really get to know someone, there must be intimacy. Truthfully speaking, many would choose rather not to know God, but to live a 'blessed' life. Many would also say that it does not take all of this. They would rather have the blessings of God and not the character and the presence of God. When you are in a relationship where the character and the presence of God does not exist, there is also no peace, joy, or righteousness prevailing in that atmosphere. Therefore, many people who have money without a right relationship with God or man are miserable. Anyone can put on a front, pretending to be happy, but if you spend time with someone who is void of the character and presence of God, you will find out that they were just overcompensating in many ways to cover up their unhappiness. Many people want the manifestation without a personal relationship with Jesus Christ. They want the promise without going through the pain. If you ask any one if they want to be blessed of course the answer would be yes. On the other hand, if you asked how many wanted to suffer for the blessing, many would say no. God has left us a promise that the suffering will never outweigh the blessings.

Romans 8:18 says, "For I reckon that the sufferings of this present time are not worthy to be compared with the glory which shall be revealed in us."

Our Spiritual Posture

Our spiritual posture is the attitude in which we position ourselves or approach God. This posture is demonstrated in how we worship and live our lives in the presence of an almighty God. This generation has become so religious in how we define our relationship with God by always casually mentioning fasting and prayer while we live lifestyles that do not exemplify a surrendered life before God. We also casually make mention of miracle, signs and wonders while not demonstrating the true essence of a move of God. If you listen to many people, some are always mentioning that they are experiencing a move of God in their churches only to find out, once you attend, that it's not only a fabricated story but a demonstration of emotionalism and a form of godliness with no real power.

But what is our spiritual posture supposed to resemble? The word of God tells us to "enter His gates with thanksgiving and to enter His courts with praise (Psalm 100:4)." Also, we don't just stop here, but we learn to "wait" on God through our worship. And to do this takes a surrendered life. David said:

Psalm 40:1-3 King - (KJV) [40] *I waited patiently for the Lord; and he inclined unto me, and heard my cry.* [2] *He brought me up also out of an horrible pit, out of the miry clay, and set my feet upon a rock, and established my goings.* [3] *And he hath put a new song in my mouth, even praise unto our God: many shall see it, and fear, and shall trust in the Lord.*

Sometimes we are waiting for something grand to happen when what we need to do is just wait in His presence. *Habakkuk (2:1) said, "I will stand upon my watch, and set me upon the tower, and will watch to see what he will say unto me, and what I shall answer when I am reproved."* Habakkuk knew what it took to wait in God's presence for Him to speak. He also made his place of waiting personal, "my watch", because this endeavor was a part of his routine when he sought the Lord. Do you have a favorite waiting place before the Lord where He meets and talk to you?

When we frequent the presence of God it becomes an expectation in our spirit, as well as with our Father.

Pregnant with Promise

If a woman says that she is pregnant, there is an expectation of a child being born, which will become the manifestation of that pregnancy. When we come into union with Christ, we become heirs to the promises of God. *Galatians 3:29: And if ye be Christ's, then are ye Abraham's seed, and heirs according to the promise.* Because of these promises, there is an expectation throughout our lifetime, for what God has spoken concerning us in His word, or even over us through prophecy, that we will someday come into manifestation. We must remember that these promises have been reserved for those who are in Christ, although, there are those who tap into the promises of God through following the principles of His word and come into great wealth, yet not having and possessing salvation or Christ-like character. Well, you may ask how does this happen? You must remember that the gifts and callings of God are without repentance *(Romans 11:29)*. You do not have to be born again to tap into great wealth, but you must be born again to go to heaven.

Philippians 3: 13, 14 - Brethren, I count not myself to have apprehended: but this one thing I do, *forgetting those things which are behind, and reaching forth unto those things which are before, ^{14}I press toward the mark for the prize of the high calling of God in Christ Jesus.*

We will never understand everything that we go through, but we cannot afford to permit that which we do not understand to hinder us from moving forward. Satan wants to stop your progression or your ability to move forward so that you never make it to manifestation. Satan is always trying to get you to give up. God has all of us on a path. This path is unique to you and is not like someone else's path. We must "know him" because he knows the way that we should take (ref. Job 23:10).

Fullness of Time

Manifestation comes only in the 'fullness of time'. For instance, the clouds that form in the sky before a storm comes become very dark and heavy before it rains. If there is an interruption in the process of this formation, the rain will not come. Many of us have experienced delays concerning the promises of God in our lives. Something or someone came along and interrupted the process *(You did run well, who did hinder you that you should not obey the truth? Gal. 5:7)*. You must recognize this was only a test that was allowed to come to make and break you and then validate your position in God. It is God's will that you come through these tests and not get stuck in these situations. I prophesy to these circumstances that they will release you and that you be made completely whole so that you can now continue on the journey that God started you on to bring you into the fulfillment of that which God has promised you.

Sometimes it may become cloudy, but it does not rain because all that needs to happen in the process has not happened. I, of course, am not a meteorologist, but this is just a simple example comparing the process of a promise coming to pass in our lives. *Galatians 4:4 But when the <u>fullness</u> of the time was come, God sent forth his Son...* God did not just send his Son at any given time. In the mind of God, everything that needed to have happened prior to that time in history, every prophecy spoken concerning Jesus Christ's coming, every preparation for this event had been fulfilled.

> *Acts 2:1 - And when the day of Pentecost was <u>fully</u> come, they were all with one accord in one place. ² And suddenly there came a sound from heaven as of a rushing mighty wind, and it filled all the house where they were sitting. ³ And there appeared unto them cloven tongues like as of fire, and it sat upon each of them. ⁴ And they were all filled with the Holy Ghost, and began to speak with other tongues, as the Spirit gave them utterance.*

Those who went into the upper room went with the expectation of continually waiting until God manifested the promised Holy Spirit. *Acts 1:14 say, "These all continued with one accord in prayer and supplication, with the women, and Mary the mother of Jesus, and with his brethren."* There must be a *continuation* until there is *manifestation*. Satan loves to bring interruptions that will ultimately stop the flow of the Holy Spirit whose will it is to bring you into the 'fullness of time" in order to manifest God's perfect will concerning you. Too many inconsistencies will eventually abort the will of God in your life, therefore you must continue in prayer, fasting, and the ministry of the Word. *Acts 13* speaks about certain prophets and teachers who came to minister before the Lord through fasting and prayer. After spending much time ministering to the Lord, there was a *manifestation* of the Spirit, the Holy Ghost saying, *"Separate me Barnabas and Saul for the work whereunto I have called them."* It is so important that we learn to stay before God until we get a manifestation. God may choose to speak to our spirits and give us direction for our lives, or even an answer to a specific prayer. Whatever the manifestation, we must learn to stay before God until the answer comes. We cannot afford to allow distractions in any form to hinder us from coming into the promises of God.

God has left us promises and has given us authority over our circumstances. It is up to us to do the rest in order to come into manifestation. He has given us mighty weapons of warfare such as fasting, prayer, and his Word to ensure our Victory!! *Isaiah 55:11 - So shall my word be that goeth forth out of my mouth: it shall not return unto me void, but it shall accomplish that which I please, and it shall prosper in the thing whereto I sent it.* I charge you this day to put in remembrance all the things that God has spoken concerning your life. It is up to you to allow God to take you through the process that will ultimately bring you into the promise that He has for your life. Remember that His Word will not return unto Him void or unfulfilled. It is not God's will for your life to become unfulfilled, but prosperous and accomplished. But it is our responsibility not to allow Satan to deceive us out of the future God has planned for us.

Examine Yourself

We must examine ourselves, because often we question God as to why we have not come into the blessings that he has promised we can have. This same question may transcend many other areas of our lives. The first thing we must do is not blame God, or even others for this matter but examine ourselves.

2 Corinthians 13:5 - Examine and test and evaluate your own selves to see whether you are holding to your faith and showing the proper fruits of it. Test and prove yourselves [not Christ]. Do you not yourselves realize and know [thoroughly by an ever-increasing experience] that Jesus Christ is in you--unless you are [counterfeits] disapproved on trial and rejected? (AMP)

The truth of the matter is that, God's Word works!!! But we must remember to work the Word. If we are coming up short correcting errors in our lives, then God expects us to first examine ourselves, through prayer and the reading of God's word, then we must repent by turning from away from sinful ways, bad habits, lack of love, lack of benevolence, or whatever God reveals to us through the mirror of His Word. Believe me, if we do not do this, there is no need for us thinking that God is going to just look the other way when we are doing wrong or going in the wrong direction and just bless us. Although this is what we sometimes expect, when we do not get what we want from God, we began to murmur and complain asking God, why? God desires to bring manifestation into all of our lives concerning the things that he has promised us; but he will not do it at the expense of going against his own Word.

Isaiah 59:1 – 2: BEHOLD, THE Lord's hand is not shortened at all, that it cannot save, nor His ear dull with deafness that it cannot hear. ²But your iniquities have made a separation between you and your God, and your sins have hidden His face from you, so that He will not hear. (AMP)

I believe that we not only sometimes murmur and complain against God, but sometimes we go looking for someone to agree with us while we are having a pity-party rather than repenting to God for our shortcomings. We see this happening with the children of Israel time and time again. When one person started murmuring and complaining, this same spirit spread through the camp like wildfire.

Numbers 14:36-37, "And the men, which Moses sent to search the land, who returned, and made all the congregation to murmur against him, by bringing up a slander upon the land, ³⁷Even those men that did bring up the evil report upon the land, died by the plague before the LORD."

God is never pleased when we do not respond correctly when he is trying to discipline us so that we will "grow up" and become mature enough to understand that He knows what is best for us. And better yet, he knows the way that we should take. In the scripture above, God was ready to bless Israel by bringing them into the promise land. They proved that they were not ready, because as soon as they faced challenges instead of them putting their trust in the God who had already provided for them and brought them up out of Egypt, they began to doubt God by murmuring and complaining. I have known people to not only throw tantrums, but also get others involved in their own disobedience. Everyone who is connected to us will suffer when we do not obey God. For instance, if you do not pay your tithes and offerings, you are not going to be fully blessed. As a matter of fact, *Malachi 3* says you are "cursed with a curse." There is no substitute for our obedience towards God. Looking for another way to get to the blessing without going through God will only get you in deep trouble. God is the one who is going to bring to pass what he has promised us. *It is not by our might, nor by power, but by his Spirit. (Ref. Zechariah 4:6)*

Time to Manifest

What are you tolerating? What type of negotiations are you making? Who are you accommodating? When is the last time you received a revelation from God? You need to be asking, where is my manifestation? If you go through life being unfruitful and never examining yourself as to why things are the way they are in your life, then you are cheating yourself out of the destiny that God has promised you can have. I don't know about you, but I want everything that God has promised me. It's time to MANIFEST!!!

The fact that God has visited this present-day church in these last days will be characterized and established by demonstrations of the Spirit of God. God promises us in *Haggai 2:9 – "The glory of this latter house shall be greater than of the former, saith the Lord of hosts."* Praise God, the "Glory" has returned to the earth and will manifest through the true sons and daughters of God! Not just in the church, but wherever we are we will manifest and demonstrate God's power. As we begin to walk in our manifested destinies, this will lead to greater demonstrations of the Spirit of God in our lives and in the marketplace. We will begin to see greater demonstrations of healing, deliverance and even wealth flowing throughout the Body of Christ. The gifts of the Spirit will increase in operation and magnitude. If you are not prepared, then it is time to get back into that place of intimacy with God through prayer, consecration, and the study and meditation of God's Word.

> *1 Corinthians 2: 4 - And my speech and my preaching was not with enticing words of man's wisdom, but in demonstration of the Spirit and of power.*

A lot of what we see today is nothing more than man's intellect on display. The power and presence of the Most High God is not in demonstration because not many are willing to pay the price. People are being enticed, entertained and financially drained by churches that have no power and presence of God in them. Many leaders are in fallen states due to compromise and the people are simply going along with the program. But God is raising up true worshippers who desire to see a move of God! These worshippers are hungry and thirsty for the presence of a living God and they will not stop seeking His face until they see manifestation!

It's time to 'Manifest!!!!"

Chapter 8

It's Your Time

"The Celebration!"

1 Peter 5:10 - But the God of all grace, who hath called us unto his eternal glory by Christ Jesus, after that ye have suffered a while, make you perfect, stablish, strengthen, settle you.

It's your time! It's your time to be celebrated, honored and acknowledged; not for your glory but for God's glory. God allowed you to be processed for His glory! But in the place, he has perfected you or brought you into maturity, He has also planted or established you. God has brought you to a place of stability to be planted on a strong foundation. God has strengthened you and caused you to come to a place where you are now healthier, wealthier and wiser. And lastly, He has settled you; brought you to a place of fulfillment, satisfaction and resolve. This place is where he has not only commanded the blessing, but a public declaration of His glory upon your life. The word of God declares that the sowing that you have done in secret will now be rewarded openly (Matt. 6:4). The tears that you have sown, the sacrifices that you have made have now come to a time and place of harvest. The word of God says that they that sow in tears shall reap in joy (Psalms 126:5-6). There is nothing on earth that will stop your time of celebration because it has been ordained by God. You have come full circle for such a time as this! God, himself, will cause you to be celebrated even in the presence of your enemies; your table has been prepared!!

Jesus Is Celebrated!

Matthew 21: ¹And when they drew nigh unto Jerusalem, and were come to Bethphage, unto the mount of Olives, then sent Jesus two disciples, ²Saying unto them, Go into the village over against you, and straightway ye shall find an ass tied, and a colt with her: loose them, and bring them unto me. ³And if any man say ought unto you, ye shall say, The Lord hath need of them; and straightway he will send them. ⁴All this was done, that it might be fulfilled which was spoken by the prophet, saying, ⁵Tell ye the daughter of Sion, Behold, thy King cometh unto thee, meek, and sitting upon an ass, and a colt the foal of an ass. ⁶And the disciples went, and did as Jesus commanded them, ⁷And brought the ass, and the colt, and put on them their clothes, and they set him thereon. ⁸And a very great multitude spread their garments in the way; others cut down branches from the trees, and strawed them in the way. ⁹And the multitudes that went before, and that followed, cried, saying, Hosanna to the son of David: Blessed is he that cometh in the name of the Lord; Hosanna in the highest. ¹⁰And when he was come into Jerusalem, all the city was moved, saying, Who is this? ¹¹And the multitude said, This is Jesus the prophet of Nazareth of Galilee.

As Jesus entered Jerusalem, remember, "It was His time to be celebrated!!! This event had to take place because it had been prophesied many years before. *Zechariah 9:9 says,*

"Rejoice greatly, O daughter of Zion; shout, O daughter of Jerusalem: behold, thy King cometh unto thee: he is just, and having salvation; lowly, and riding upon an ass, and upon a colt the foal of an ass."

It was time for Jesus to be celebrated and not everyone was willing to even celebrate the King of Kings and the Lord of Lords, so you should not be surprised when people that you know, some of who you call family and friends, are not willing to celebrate you!! But one thing I like about God is that He knows who to send into your life when it is your time!!!

Luke 19: 37-40 - [37]And when he was come nigh, even now at the descent of the mount of Olives, the whole multitude of the disciples began to rejoice and praise God with a loud voice for all the mighty works that they had seen; [38]Saying, Blessed be the King that cometh in the name of the Lord: peace in heaven, and glory in the highest. [39]And some of the Pharisees from among the multitude said unto him, Master, rebuke thy disciples. [40]And he answered and said unto them, I tell you that, if these should hold their peace, the stones would immediately cry out.

There are events that must take place in your life, if you are obedient, because these things were prophesied over you many years before. We should ever keep the words that were spoken over our lives in remembrance. We should also begin to cry out to God concerning these things in our prayers. The words of prophecy spoken over us have a direct impact on our destinies. Words have a very powerful influence over our lives. Words that are spoken to us will eventually direct our belief system and guide us into our destiny. *Proverbs 18:21 says, "Death and life are in the power of the tongue: and they that love it shall eat the fruit thereof."* As stated earlier, it is so important that we surround ourselves with the right kind of people. No one wants to walk alone, but in some seasons of your life, it may be necessary. Sometimes it can be so hard finding someone to agree with you about what God said about your life. When this happens, you are forced to agree alone with what God has said about you, whether it is through prophecy or what you have read in the Word of God. Also remember that whether or not you are celebrated has a lot to do with the choices you make in life. There was a time when Jesus went into a town and could not work miracles, not because he did not have the power, but because the people did not believe in him. *Matthew 13:57 says, "And they were offended in* him. But Jesus said unto them, *"A prophet is not without honor, save in his own country, and in his own house." "⁵⁸And he did not many mighty works there because of their unbelief."* On the other hand, there were those who simply heard that Jesus was passing by, believed and were healed, delivered and set free.

> *Luke 18: ³⁵ And it came to pass, that as he was come nigh unto Jericho, a certain blind man sat by the way side begging: ³⁶And hearing the multitude pass by, he asked what it meant. ³⁷And they told him, that Jesus of Nazareth passeth by. ³⁸And he cried, saying, Jesus, thou son of David, have mercy on me. ³⁹And they which went before rebuked him, that he should hold his peace: but he cried so much the more, Thou son of David, have mercy on me. ⁴⁰And Jesus stood, and commanded him to be brought unto him: and when he was come near, he asked him, ⁴¹Saying, what wilt thou that I shall do unto thee? And he said, Lord, that I may receive my sight. ⁴²And Jesus said unto him, Receive thy sight: thy faith hath saved thee. ⁴³And immediately he received his sight, and followed him, glorifying God: and all the people, when they saw it, gave praise unto God.*

The possibilities are great when you are surrounded by people who agree with you, have faith in you, and believe that God has both called and anointed you. But when people do not know you by the spirit of God, there is no connection, no agreement then doubts will arise when you began to share your purpose with them. *Genesis 37:5 says, "And Joseph dreamed a dream, and he told it his brethren: and they hated him yet the more."* It is so important to be around people who will celebrate your purpose. These people are not jealous when God blesses and promotes you. Aren't you tired of being tolerated? We can choose who we allow to enter our lives. Remember that God gave us the power to bind and loose. If you choose to remain amid people who will only tolerate you, then you will notice that your life and abilities are being limited by your surroundings. When Jesus saw the unbelief of the people in his town, he left and went to another people who believed that he was anointed to do the works that God had sent him to do. I don't know about you, but I do not have time to sit around trying to convince people that God has called me do to something, and I refuse to allow people to hinder and rob me of my blessings. It is my time and it is your time to be celebrated!!

Called Out

Sometimes the unbelief that you are surrounded by is so bad, that God must take you out of that environment not only to bless you but to ultimately bring you into the destiny he has promised. In the case with Abraham God removed him from the midst of his people as soon as he revealed that he was going to bless him.

Genesis 12: ¹Now the LORD had said unto Abram, Get thee out of thy country, and from thy kindred, and from thy father's house, unto a land that I will shew thee: ²And I will make of thee a great nation, and I will bless thee, and make thy name great; and thou shalt be a blessing: ³And I will bless them that bless thee, and curse him that curseth thee: and in thee shall all families of the earth be blessed. ⁴So Abram departed, as the LORD had spoken unto him; and Lot went with him: and Abram was seventy and five years old when he departed out of Haran.

I believe with all my heart that God not only wants to bless us, but we tie his hands when we are not able to discern his voice and directions for our lives. God looks down and sees all the things that will sabotage the blessings that he desires to bestow upon us. His command to us is to come up higher and began to soar with eagle's wings in the spirit so that we can see what he sees and hear more clearly his voice.

If you notice in the beginning of Genesis Chapter 12, the Lord tells Abram to leave his family behind. But in disobedience to God, he takes his nephew Lot, which later proves to be a big mistake. Abram, later called Abraham, had problems with Lot time and time again from having to go into battles to rescue him to also having to rescue him from Sodom & Gomorrah. Lastly, there was strife between Abraham's herdsmen and Lot's herdsmen, and this is where they separated. After Lot separated from Abraham, God once again began to speak to him concerning the promise.

> *Genesis 13:14 (KVJ) - And the LORD said unto Abram, after that Lot was separated from him, Lift up now thine eyes, and look from the place where thou art northward, and southward, and eastward, and westward.*

This had to be confirmed to Abraham in the absence of Lot, because the promise was not made to Lot, but to Abraham. From this account we understand the following:

- Lot represents those relationships that are "familiar (family) but disrespectful"
- Lot represents "the opportunists" – Lot didn't want a relationship with God but the blessings of God
- Lot represents "wrong motives" – Connected for all the wrong reasons
- Lot represents "dream thieves" – Wanted to illegally obtain Abraham's purpose and blessings. Leave Lot at Home.

Once you have dealt with these areas in your life, you are now ready to be blessed and celebrated!!!! The people who are coming to the celebration are those who are ordained to be a part of your life and ministry. No one who is invited is sad or jealous because you are being celebrated but everyone at your party has brought you a gift, and not one is empty handed. It is terrible when you invite someone to a party and they are not only empty handed, but only came to eat, freeload, beg, and see what others have brought. God only promises to bless givers, for his word says he will give seed to the sower. *2 Corinthians 9:10 say "Now he that ministereth seed to the sower both minister bread for your food, and multiply your seed sown, and increase the fruits of your righteousness."* They are even ready to become the cheerleaders at your celebrations because they *know it's your time. It's your time!!!* God bless those people who have an ear to hear what the spirit has to say to them. *Luke 6:31 - And as ye would that men should do to you, do ye also to them likewise.* It is the heart of God in manifestation when we can love our neighbors as ourselves. Some people only love themselves, and they do not know properly how to do that!!! The word plainly tells us that in the last days men would be lovers of themselves.

> *2 Timothy 3: [1]This know also, that in the last days perilous times shall come. [2]For men shall be lovers of their own selves, covetous, boasters, proud, blasphemers, disobedient to parents, unthankful, unholy, [3]Without natural affection, trucebreakers, false accusers, incontinent, fierce ,despisers of those that are good, [4]Traitors, heady, high-minded, lovers of pleasures more than lovers of God; [5]Having a form of godliness, but denying the power thereof: from such turn away.*

God says to turn away from people who claim to be "Christians" but have the wrong type of fruit growing in their lives. They are forever learning about God and becoming more religious but are never coming into the knowledge of the truth. I would rather sit and eat with sinners who want to better their lives but have not learned about the grace of God, than to sit with the religious in their pretty church outfits but are becoming rotten even while on the tree. God's command and plan is for us to come into maturity so that we can love one another and not just think about ourselves. I know that all of us were once hurting, broke, and disgusted, but for those who want to come into maturity and perfection, this is when you give to others or sow into someone's life. Let's Celebrate!!

> *Philippians 2: [1]If there be therefore any consolation in Christ, if any comfort of love, if any fellowship of the Spirit, if any bowels and mercies, [2]Fulfil ye my joy, that ye be likeminded, having the same love, being of one accord, of one mind. [3]Let nothing be done through strife or vainglory; but in lowliness of mind let each esteem other better than themselves. [4]Look not every man on his own things, but every man also on the things of others. [5]Let this mind be in you, which was also in Christ Jesus:*

We can pout and throw all the tantrums we want to, but unless we do things God's way, change will not occur in our favor. Remember the children of Israel pouted and refused to grow up, but their tantrums never changed God's requirements for them. Even after wandering in the desert for 40 years, they refused to change and were cut off. Only Joshua and Caleb from that company of people entered the Promised Land because they followed all of God's commands wholeheartedly.

As God prepares you for his promises, there are some who are being invited to come to your celebration. They will either be qualified because their hearts are properly positioned toward God and man or disqualified because of disobedience. In order to be qualified, you must love others more than yourself. To better describe the attributes of being qualified let's read.

> *Romans 12: ⁹Let love be without dissimulation. Abhor that which is evil; cleave to that which is good. ¹⁰Be kindly affectioned one to another with brotherly love; in honour preferring one another; ¹¹Not slothful in business; fervent in spirit; serving the Lord; ¹²Rejoicing in hope; patient in tribulation; continuing instant in prayer; ¹³Distributing to the necessity of saints; given to hospitality. ¹⁴Bless them which persecute you: bless, and curse not. ¹⁵Rejoice with them that do rejoice, and weep with them that weep. ¹⁶Be of the same mind one toward another. Mind not high things but condescend to men of low estate. Be not wise in your own conceits. ¹⁷Recompense to no man evil for evil. Provide things honest in the sight of all men. ¹⁸If it be possible, as much as lieth in you, live*

peaceably with all men. ¹⁹Dearly beloved, avenge not yourselves, but rather give place unto wrath: for it is written, Vengeance is mine; I will repay, saith the Lord. ²⁰Therefore if thine enemy hunger, feed him; if he thirst, give him drink: for in so doing thou shalt heap coals of fire on his head. ²¹Be not overcome of evil but overcome evil with good.

It is about high time to realize that religiously following God by being just hearers of the word of God and not doers is not working in our lives. If we do not learn to practice the word of God in our everyday lives, we will continue be defeated rather than being the overcomers God has created us to be. From the example of the children of Israel, we should know that it is going to be God's way or no way. It is so important that we understand what God is doing in our lives and know who God is sending to us in this season. *It's time for the celebration!*

Prophetic Release – God is sending you in a new direction and you will be connected to a new people. God will not put new wine into old wineskins, nor will He put a new move of God into something that He has declared ICHABOD. But He will do a new thing in your life through a new people in a new place and you will see the manifestation of God and be celebrated, and God will get the glory!

www.ingramcontent.com/pod-product-compliance
Lightning Source LLC
Chambersburg PA
CBHW070510100426
42743CB00010B/1799